BizWorld

How to Create an Irresistible Business Universe
Your Customers Love to Buy from
and Hate to Leave

By Ben Settle

Ben Settle

Whoa!

What in the World Do You
Think You're Doing?

Before taking even one single step further, grab your complementary issue of the prestigious *Email Players Newsletter* at the link below. You'll also get access to the dozens of hours of advanced audio/video training inside the free Ben Settle mobile app — all of which can be used to help nab your business even more engagement, more sales, and more influence.

BenSettle.com

Ben Settle

How to Avoid Creating a World of Legal Hurt for Yourself

Marketing World Conqueror

Since 2002 Ben Settle has curated marketing strategies, copywriting campaigns, & email sequences for clients & his own businesses that have collectively helped earn tens of millions of dollars in sales in hyper competitive, "cutthroat" markets such as golf, weight loss, biz op, self-defense, home business, dating, prostate problems, internet marketing, and more.

Ben has also taught methods he's pioneered to some of the world's most respected & successful direct marketing companies—such as Agora Financial... AWAI's popular Copywriting Bootcamp events & Wealthy Web Writer series... professional radio producers at Entercom (one of the largest radio broadcasting companies in the United States)... Brian Kurtz's Titans Masterclasses... Real Dose's (one of the world's biggest and most respected health supplement companies) Health Profits Summit... the late Clayton Makepeace's private mastermind... various seminars & events where people pay up to $10k just for a seat... and the Oceans 4 Mastermind—where 7, 8, & 9 figure businesses paid him and his pals to put their marketing on the "hot seat"—transforming their sales overnight.

In addition, Ben publishes the prestigious Email Players Newsletter read by hundreds of business owners in 50+ countries—including by A-list copywriters, leaders at powerful direct marketing companies like Agora Financial, New York Times best-selling authors, & more.

Most recently he's been investing in cutting edge software for email marketing, social media, internet marketing, content creation, & mobile apps.

What the Marketing World's Elites Say…

"Good copy intoxicates me. Yours is high proof. I'm enjoying it."
- Gary Bencivenga
www.MarketingBullets.com

"I think Ben is the light heavyweight champion of email copywriting. I also think we'd make Mayweather money in a unification title bout!"
- Matt Furey
www.MattFurey.com

"Ben is one of the sharpest marketing minds on the planet, and he runs his membership *Email Players* better than just about any other I've seen. I highly recommend it."
- Perry Marshall
www.PerryMarshall.com

"I love your emails. Your e-mail style is stunningly effective."
- Bob Bly
www.Bly.com

"I've been a big admirer of Ben's writing, he's the only copywriter I've hired and been satisfied with."
- Ken McCarthy
www.KenMcCarthy.com

"…you have some of the best hooks. You really know how to work the hook and the angles."
- Brian Clark

www.CopyBlogger.com

"Of all the people I follow, there's so much stuff that comes into my inbox…your stuff is as good as it gets."
  - Brian Kurtz
  www.BrianKurtz.me

"I start my day with reading from the Holy Bible and Ben Settle's email, not necessarily in that order."
  - Richard Armstrong
  www.FreeSampleBook.com

"You're damn brilliant, dude…I really *do* admire your work, my friend!"
  - Brian Keith Voiles

"Ben has such a strong and well-defined brand, that the designs practically create themselves."
  - Kia Arian
  www.ZineGraphics.com

"Love or hate him, you won't ignore him. And ultimately his message is delivered with such a wallop of whoop-ass'ing truth you can't help but buy what he's selling."
  - Keith Commins
  www.PearlDesign.ie

"I'm so busy but there're some guys like Ben Settle with incredible daily emails that I always read."
  - Russell Brunson
  www.RussellBrunson.com

"You are saying, in very arresting ways, things I've been trying to teach marketers and copywriters for 30 years. Keep up the good work!"
  - Mark Ford
  Co-founder of AWAI

"Ben has written sales letters for us that have resulted in millions of dollars for us. And probably tens of millions of dollars in ongoing and repeat sales. He's also been one of the most liked and well received speakers and presenters at our No Excuses Summit."
  - Tim Erway
  www.EliteMarketingPro.com

"The business is so big now. Prob 4x the revenue since when we first met…
and had you in! Claim credit, as it did correlate!"
  - Joseph Schriefer
  Agora Financial Copy Chief

"I wake up to *read your words*. I learn from you and study exactly how you
combine words + feelings together. Like no other. *You* go *deep* and *hard*."
  - Lori Haller
  www.ShadowOakStudio.com

"…I get great advice and at least one chuckle… or a slap on the forehead
'duh'… every time I read your emails!"
  - Carline Anglade-Cole
  www.CarlineCole.com

"The f'in' hottest email copywriter on the web."
  - David Garfinkel
  The World's Greatest Copywriting Coach
  www.CopywritersPodcast.com

"Ben writes some of the most compelling subject lines I've ever seen, and
implements a very unique style in his blog. I can't help but look when I get
an email from him."
  - Dr. Glenn Livingston
  www.GlennLivingston.com

"Your emails are one of the very few I read and study. And your laid-back
style... is just perfect!"
  - Ryan Lee
  www.RyanLee.com

"Ben's emails are perfect examples of how to sell with email and how to
create a persona that draws people to you like controversy to Donald Trump"
  - David Deutsch
  www.DavidLDeutsch.com

"Ben is the dude to study if you want to write powerful emails that make a
bunch of money."
  - Doberman Dan Gallapoo
  www.DobermanDan.com

"There's been a recent flood of copy writing 'gurus' lately and I only trust *one!*
And that's @BenSettle"

- Bryan Sharpe
www.BooksByBryan.com

"Ben Settle is my email marketing mentor."
- Tom Woods
www.TomWoods.com

World Atlas of Contents

Introduction: A "Quickie" Crash Course in Business World-Building

True story:

Many years ago, a woman named Natasa Lekic, CEO of a New York firm that helps authors create a book and then connects them with sought-after editors in the industry, sent me an email that said two things:

1. She's not a fan of my emails.

2. But she read my *Zombie Cop* novel (the first book in my Enoch Wars series), said it was good, and has a great sense of pacing and World-Building. She even graciously offered to connect me with an agent. (That's not what her company does—so nothing in it for her.)

Anyway, that got me thinking about something hardly any other marketers think about.

And that is the idea of World-Building.

To me, it's very natural after mindlessly spending my youth in cahoots with a couple other kids who also had no other friends or lives playing Dungeons & Dragons and other RPG's. Building worlds, characters, adventures, narratives, and story arcs come naturally from that.

And it was just as natural to bring that to my marketing.

And to my brand.

And, yes, to my business as a whole.

Like, for example:

When I ran an insanely addictive—according to many of its members, at least—Facebook group called *elBenbo's Lair*. I built a "world" full of surprises, rules, laws, languages, customs, characters, storylines, plot twists, and other such hijinks that made it, so it wasn't unusual to have someone call it "real life" with everything outside the group being ignored. Sometimes there were so many concurrent Thread-holes, discussions, debates, and arguments going on people would post stuff on their main timeline they'd rather the public not see, thinking they were safely in my group, only to have their friends and family think they let the cuckoo out of the clock.

Such was the power of building my own world.

Here's something else:

I once taught this topic to Email Players subscriber Brian Kurtz's prestigious Mastermind.

And it's like I told them:

In my experience, World-Building can not only create legions of fans and customers and potentially make your business all-but "cancel-proof"... but it can also help grow a business where making sales can become easy and automatic versus a constant struggle and chore—endlessly trying to gamify, hack, and manipulate your way into peoples wallets. World-Building can mean having a place people want to be and fight to stay inside of, instead a place you need to desperately try to keep people from leaving.

In other words:

It's a *privilege* to be in your World, not a right.

It's also an adventure from their boring lives.

And, yes, it can be a platform unto itself.

Do it right and in essence you can become your own Platform.

That is why I believe—even after your death, if you do World-Building correctly—your business can never be truly cancelled, de-platformed, suppressed, manipulated, or controlled by some overreaching big tech or government entity.

And perhaps best of all:

World-Building—again, when done right—means putting your business in a position where you are not being pushy or selling as much as you are giving customers the opportunity to buy. World-Building can give you the kind of super tight bond with your fans, customers, clients, and audience no other "marketer" screwing around on Facebook and obsessing over a spreadsheet can ever hope to have. Especially as they reactively spank out their silly little offers while bragging and virtue signaling about nonsense in a desperate attempt to try to stay relevant—lucky to get even a fraction of the engagement, response, and sales you can get if you but build a world people want to inhabit, stay in, and buy within.

In a word, World-Building equals what I have heard Dan Kennedy describe as:

"Omnipresence."

In my way of thinking the best way to have Omnipresence is to be omnipresent.

And in my opinion and experience:

The best way to do that is a World people want to be in their every waking hour.

More:

You can't "swipe" World-Building from someone else. As I've had to tell a few people, I can't even show examples of it outside of observing what they see me doing. It's like saying, "Look at Disney, that's World-Building!" without any context, because there are thousands of variables—all unique just to Walt in many cases—involved.

Same with other great World-builders both dead and alive.

It ain't something you look at and extract lessons from piecemeal.

It's something you look at as a whole.

Especially when you understand the main intricacies of how it works.

Still more:

This is not something you build in a day or a month. It requires literally months and years of thinking about it, applying it, and growing it. You start with one "cog" in your world, and build from there. And even then, it is never really "finished" if you are doing it right.

In other words:

Ain't no checklist for how to do it.

And no feedback is required.

Building a world transcends feedback.

And probably a lot of feedback should be ignored anyway.

It's *your* world, not whoever is giving you feedback's world, after all.

I can't speak for any of these guys, but Walt Disney, Steve Jobs, Fred Rogers, Jim Henson, and the handful of other businesses I've observed who have done it, very likely did not seek "feedback." They almost certainly just did it intuitively, based on a whole host of factors and preferences and goals and motivations unique to them, and them alone—plus knowledge of their markets, industries, and lists.

Bottom line:

If it was "simple and easy!" then everyone would do it.

Which is exactly why everyone won't or can't do it. Especially those who struggle with original, strategic, creative, and/or long-term thinking. Or those who need a checklist for everything. Or who can't make a move without consulting their Facebook friends, their life coach, or their horoscope.

It certainly won't be something anyone lacking patience can do.

Which brings me to this book.

I've been asked to teach this topic for years. And I have done so in various high-ticket books, masterminds, and coaching programs. This book is a compilation of all the best trainings from these platforms, gathered together, in one place. Just realize you will notice repetition of ideas, thoughts, and strategies. And that is by design. World-Building isn't rocket science, and there aren't all that many moving parts. But what it does require is mastery of the fundamentals, developing a gut feeling for what your market wants, and a lot of deep, strategical thinking. It takes a lot of patience, too. As this isn't a checklist of short-term tricks and tactics you can run off and test. It's a lifelong journey you'll be on for many years to come. And, if you do it right, it'll still grow long after you shuffle off your mortal coil and join the choir invisible.

All right, one last thing, and it's important:

This is not a perfectly written and structured book, and is almost entirely in transcript form, except for the appendices, which are from certain books I've written. If reading transcripts gives you heartburn realize you'd have to pay upwards of ten thousand dollars to access all the trainings this book is made up of. For example, one of them is part of a $19k per year mastermind I taught at. Another is part of a $500/month coaching program I co-created. And still others are from books I've written that costs several hundred dollars—not to mention the time you'd have to spend finding, gathering, and parsing some of the podcasts I pulled some of the other chapters from.

So, a word of warning:

Because it's in transcript form this book probably has a lot of grammar and spelling problems. After all, it was me talking, not writing. And no human being that isn't a sociopathic robot speaks in perfect, grammatically correct syntax. And while I did my best to clean up some of the rough parts, it's going to have some grammar and spelling snafus here and there.

Another word of warning:

As I mentioned, you will no doubt notice there is a lot of repetition of ideas in this book. Remember, that is by design. The more you imbibe and think about what you see repeated (the stories, analogies, etc.) the faster learning, implementing, and profiting from this book should be.

All right so that's that.

To begin your BizWorld journey turn the page and dig in…

The Lost Art of World-Building in Business

Presentation about World-Building at Brian Kurtz's
prestigious Titans of Direct Response Mastermind

BRIAN KURTZ: Welcome, Ben. It's great to see you. You have been someone that this group has asked to have speak on numerous occasions. Not that you were so elusive to me. I know you don't speak a lot and you consider yourself the reclusive hermit. But I think that I guess I just had to ask, and you said yes, and that was just fantastic, so I really appreciate you being here.

So, I think originally, Ben was going to do a presentation called *Email Armageddon*, which sounded really intense. And it was too intense for this session because you said it was going to be too long.

BEN SETTLE: It would have been four hours long. And even this one I'm going to try to get it into an hour. It transcends just email. It goes beyond that.

BRIAN KURTZ: All right. The title is *The Lost Art of World-Building in Business*. As he always does, he'll combine strategy with tactics. So, Ben, take it away.

BEN SETTLE: Okay. So, this is not necessarily specifically about email, and yet it has everything to do with email and it certainly has everything to do with how I do email. It can take whatever email you're doing, but not just email, anything else you're doing, and just supercharge it to the point where it almost becomes an afterthought. Because if you do the World-Building stuff right, everything else just falls into place.

This is going to be a 101 training because it's not something I hear a lot of people talk about, this idea of World-Building. It's not something I even talk a lot about and I've been doing it for 20 years. The goal here is just to get you thinking differently.

If all that happens at the end is everybody is thinking a little bit differently and a little bit bigger and more dramatically about what you're already doing, because you're already probably doing things that can work within this, I've done my job.

So, I didn't really think about this consciously several years ago, even though I've been doing it for over 20 years. When I published my first novel, which is called *Zombie Cop*, so that kind of gives you an idea of the stuff I'm interested in.

About a month after I published it, I got this email from a CEO of a New York firm that what they do is connect authors to editors. Now, I already have an editor. I'm self-published and all that. She wasn't trying to sell me anything. It's not even what her job is. She's not trying to sell me anything, she just wanted to let me know two things.

The first thing she let me know is the one thing you never really want to hear if you send emails every day, and she goes, "I really don't like your emails." And then the second thing she goes, "But, I read your *Zombie Cop* novel and it has really good pacing and World-Building." And I got to thinking and I'm like, "That comes very, very natural for me because I spent most of my childhood living in my head, building worlds, playing Dungeons & Dragons, and RPGs." It's just what I was interested in—reading fantasy novels and all that kind of stuff. World-Building is baked into this sort of thing. To me, it was the most natural thing in the world to apply this to business.

When I got into business and marketing, and copywriting, and later into email and all that, it wasn't something I did consciously, but it was definitely a part of it. I would always have these little pockets of customers that you could identify them as one of my people very easily. And that was a function of them being in my, for lack of a better word, World. I like to build worlds. That's what I do.

I'll talk about this more later, but I don't build a business, I'm building a world, which is full of characters, and narratives, and story arcs sometimes, and all kinds of crazy stuff I'll get into. It was just very natural to apply this. And nowadays, I realize it's the beating heart of everything I do. In fact, it really occurred to me when I started writing my *elBenbo Press* book about my publishing model, how just closely ingrained this is.

I did some stuff in social media where I took this to a level that was beyond obscene. I wrote about that in my Social Lair book, and I'll talk more about that. But during this time, I've learned that when you understand World-Building and when you really get it, and you get it at a level that it just becomes automatic, then sales become automatic. Getting customers becomes automatic. Getting clients becomes automatic.

You have people that want to be in your world and they don't want to leave your world. You bring them in, they don't want to go. And sometimes you have to eject people from there because they don't belong in your world. And this has created what I call berserker customers, which is a name I didn't think about until I realized I literally have customers who go ouththere and "berserk" for me. They buy everything I sell. They do everything I tell them to do. They fight battles on my behalf. They fight trolls on my behalf. They fight bad reviews on my behalf. They advocate on my behalf. They teach or they try to teach what I do on my behalf. They like to try to interpret what I do and say and spread the word. They're more like fanzines and fan fiction than actual reality in a few cases, but this is what's going on. They're just the best customers you can ask for.

I've also realized World-Building can potentially make you cancel proof. A lot of people are worried about being canceled and rightfully so. People and businesses are getting canceled all over the place right now. And not just politically conservative people in businesses, but even James Carville, the Clinton strategist guy, was just recently saying ... And to me, he's like a clock that's broken, where he's right twice per day. He said something very interesting. He said, "Everyone I talk to, even on my side of things is scared to death of being canceled by calling out the wrong things." You can witness this if you're paying attention. There's people looking to bring people down and businesses down for whatever reason. A world can't really be canceled. The business can be canceled. You could be canceled, but if you build a world, that really can't be canceled.

That's why I found making sales becomes automatic. It's not usually this constant struggle. I don't worry about, "Oh, I have a launch. I need to make so many sales!" I don't worry about any of that. Offers are often sold before you even create them if you do it right. It's a very, very interesting phenomenon you just have to experience. I hope all of you start playing with this as soon as we're done here today. Because it changes everything. And it's not complicated.

Probably the most important thing it does is, it just gives people an adventure from their boring lives. Everybody is bored. People are sitting there addicted to their phones all day because they're bored. They're looking for some kind of stimulation. Well, you get to be that stimulation. Your business gets to be that stimulation. And it doesn't matter what marketing media you use to sell with or distribute content with.

And it gives you what I've heard Dan Kennedy talk about called Omnipresence. You get to be omnipresent. When you build a world and you bring people in and they don't want to leave, you are always omnipresent. It's funny because I got some customers who work for the various Agora divisions and some of them will say, "Yeah, Ben, I read your newsletter. I'm not even subscribed." I'm like, "Well, how do you do that?" They go, "Well, people just leave your newsletters littered around the office." That's them in my world, whether they realize it or not. It brings them in. I'm omnipresent with those specific guys.

The way I see it, if you want to be omnipresent, and this may sound like a very captain obvious thing, just be omnipresent. And the way to be omnipresent is to build a world where people just want to constantly be there as often as they can during every waking hour. And I would even argue, they're non-waking hours, too, if you're doing it right.

I'm going to give one warning here and I will bring this up again later because of the nature of the business we're all in, which is direct marketing. There's no checklist for this. I would love to hand people a checklist. I've been asked for it, "Ben, show me a checklist…" No. There's no checklist for this. There's nothing to swipe either. In fact, all that stuff will just kill you with World-Building. It's something completely different. And this is very much a one-on-one thing. But realize, it comes from within. It transcends marketing by itself. It's something completely different.

Now, probably the best way I can explain this is with something Stephen King said in an interview to NPR. I'm not Stephen King's biggest fan, but I do think he's done a great job at World-Building in his novels. He talked about this from a writing point of view. I'm just going to quote it real quick.

> "20 hours a day, I live in the same reality that everyone else lives in. But for four hours a day, things change. I'm going to leave the ordinary world for my own world. And it's a wonderful, exhilarating experience. I'm very grateful to be able to have it."

Now flip that around and apply that to your customers. How can you do that for them, where they live in the ordinary world part of the time, but the rest of their time, they're in your world? And that's how you want to look at things. You want to apply this to your audiences in your list. You want your lists and your fans and your audience to leave their reality and be in your reality instead, something you've created, and of course it's business related. And in my opinion, you want them in there not just for a few hours a day, but all day. I want people in my world 24/7 to the extent that's possible. And it is possible, because I've done it. And I'm not saying I've done it with a lot of people, but when you do this right, they're in your world constantly. And I would further say you're doing them a real service as long as you're not doing nefarious things, it's actually a good thing. Hopefully that makes sense of what all this means on a practical level, but that's how I think about it.

Now, I want to give an example and then I'm going to get more into how to think about this and how to apply it to your own stuff. I think of every media that I sell in, from email to mobile apps, to social media, to direct mail, whatever it is—every media, when I do this, and I'm doing this right now, is I think of them all as different societies in my world. Right now, you're watching this, you're in one of my societies. You may not stay here. You may say, "I don't want to be here." You may click away. You may defy Brian and just turn off your camera and say, "This Ben is so full of crap. I don't want to hear anything else this guy has to say." That's fine. That's part of what happens if you're doing it right. But probably the most extreme example of what I am talking about was this old Facebook group.

Now, I have not been on Facebook since 2018. I got off there. I deleted Facebook. But when I was on Facebook, I had this thing called elBenbo's Lair. That was the name of the group. And everything I'm about to say applies to pretty much anything else. I'm just using elBenbo's Lair as an example. It was a society within my world, and it was full of surprises. And I had rules and I had laws. We had our own lexicon. We literally had our own language in there. I built a language in there. I had somebody keep taking notes on it and building it.

We had so much activity going on in there at any given time that I had to have a scribe. Like I called her a scribe who would go through all the posts every day, just to summarize them for newer people who came in, because it was just so crazy. I turned people into characters, gave them roles to play... it was a social experiment. I totally admit it. I launched a book about this called Social Lair, teaching the methodology I created from the experience.

I had storylines like soap opera storylines going on in there. I created literal soap opera storylines they thought was real. For me, it was just satire and infotainment. It was a weird thing. That was a good thing, because that's how I found Stefania. It's not like it's just all business, and it's the reason I have a teething eight-month-old right now. Brian, you said it's early for me. It's actually kind of late in the day for me. I've been up since midnight. It's fine with me. 6:30 works.

It wasn't unusual in there, because people were so ingrained in my world and they all came from my email list. I never built that group "from" Facebook. I never once told my main Facebook audience to go into this group. It was totally built from my email list. I call it email list laundering, and it's a whole other topic for creating a super curated audience using an email list and a social media page. That's a whole different topic, but it really made them better buyers and better customers.

They were all in there and they started calling it real life, because they spent so much time in there. They spent every waking minute they could in there. It got to the point where people were posting so much and rapid replying to things so much that they would get put in Facebook jail, because Facebook assumed they were bots. They were like, "Wow, this is actually my real life right now." They would go in there and there would be so much stuff going on, they didn't know if they were on their main timeline or if they're in my group to the point where some people would post stuff thinking they were in the group, but they maybe didn't want the real world to see. And only to have their family say, "What is wrong with you?" It was like that kind of thing.

It was just a very, very rabid place to be. And it was a world unto itself. I would say it was a platform unto itself. And the reason I'm bringing this up is because I want you to understand how easy sales can be made regardless of what you're selling. My current business partner in my software ventures is Troy Broussard. A couple years before we got in the software business together, we decided to do an event. We called it Wine Villains. It was held at a winery. And it wasn't supposed to be anything big or special. Maybe 10 people, I was thinking we would just have some fun, and it would make enough money to pay for the expenses for us to be there.

With maybe two or three posts just telling people about it and maybe two or three emails to my list, which I don't think actually made any of the sales, it got standing room only sold out within a couple days, six months in advance. And it wasn't because, "Oh Ben, we all want to see you, or we want to know what you're going to teach!" We actually told them, "We don't even know what we're going to teach there." We had no idea. There was no sales page for it. There was no sales letter. There wasn't even an order form. In fact, the call to action was just, "Text Troy's phone" so he could call them back and just get their order details. There was no selling involved. It was like they just wanted to be there. And it was one of those things where he's done a lot of selling. And he's like, "Ben, that was the easiest selling I've ever done." I don't know what we charged. Maybe $300 or $400 to go. Plus, some of them were traveling from different countries to be there, so it was not a cheap thing overall. He goes, "I didn't have to sell anything. I talked to them, they said, how do I do this? How do I sign up?" The result was Troy sold more people than who actually called him because he'd say, "Well, do you want to bring a spouse?" And now that spouse is being brought into the world and they came because they too wanted to be in the world I built.

Yeah, they probably wanted to hang out with me or whatever. But I think mostly they wanted to hang out with each other because they all got to know each other so well in my world. They were part of the same world. They knew each other. They knew things about each other probably their own best friends didn't know. That was the selling environment due to my World-Building. Sales were made automatically. There was no real selling—all because of the World-Building.

And this happens on my email list too, because I take this World-Building approach. I sell things and it kind of pisses me off because I spent all this time writing a sales letter, and I know they're not even reading the damn thing, because they buy right when the email goes out. And they didn't even know I was launching something. They say "I just want to have it" because they're in the world. I mean some people read it word for word. But with an awful lot of them I am thinking, "Didn't you read this? Didn't you read all this stuff after all this time I put into writing it?"

I've had people buy the same products two or three times when I'd launch something. I'm like, "You know you already have this." Then they say, "Oh, yeah, I'm sorry. Yeah, you're right. I just wanted to have it because you were selling it." For $500, $600, $800 books. Point is, is that's what happens when you build a world. It's so weird teaching this, I think, to a direct marketing crowd because I'm a direct marketer through and through. I consider myself an email supremacist. To me, that's the supreme marketing media right now that I use, at least. I use a lot of different medias, including direct mail and everything, but just email has always been the thing.

But I got to say, this World-Building is really doing most of the heavy lifting. It's doing most of the work and it's not something that's easily quantified. I can't track things very easily with this, because sales have been made sometimes before offers are even created. Those tickets at *Wine Villains*, they were sold probably years in advance in some cases. If you really think about it, they're people that just wanted to go to something, because they'd been in my world for so long, and there it was.

When I do launches and affiliate promos, I mean Brian, you know it, I sell your stuff and it usually does very well. Even the Titans stuff, which my list is small compared to some of these other guys who were selling. And I outsell all of them, yet it's not because, "Oh, I'm this genius email guy." I don't argue if someone wants to call me that, of course. But really, I built a world. I built a world and it's just a very unique place, I think, that's different from other people's businesses and the experiences they give people.

BRIAN KURTZ: Just to give a number on that. So, you doubled the amount of orders of a $2,000 product to what GKIC sold, and their list was probably 100,000.

BEN SETTLE: When I did that, my list was significantly smaller too the first time. That was probably half the size it is now, which is nowhere near 100,000 people. And it's because of a world. As you, it's one of those products that probably doesn't appeal to a lot of internet marketers. It's more for old school marketing geeks like me, for example. We love that kind of stuff. I love looking at the direct mail stuff. But most people on my list are not like that. They just want to buy something because they're in my world, and I understood how they thought. I would say in a lot of ways, this transcends technique, tactics, and even strategy. It's almost like a blend of everything, and it just takes all the stuff you're already doing and supercharges it.

And that's what I was trying to say from the beginning. You could apply all this to email. Absolutely, I do every day, but it transcends email. It transcends media. That's why when the next new media comes out, whatever that's going to be... There's always some new thing coming out. Mobile apps is new. I think it's the new internet, personally. But either way, there will be something that replaces the internet as the main thing and something that replaces mobile. Over the next 100 years, whatever. But what won't change is World-Building. It's very powerful.

Again, I have to repeat there's no checklist for this. What I can do is I can give you a beacon, I can give you metaphor and that's what I'm really going to give you here. I don't even know how you would give a checklist for this. In fact, a checklist would be the antithesis of what it makes it work.

Now, hopefully... and I went on a little limb here when I prepared this... I hope most of you are at least familiar with C. S. Lewis and his Chronicles of Narnia stories. You don't have to have read the books, but if you read the books or watched the movies, you're okay. If you haven't, I still think most of this will be self-explanatory. C.S. Lewis was a master world builder, and I use Narnia as a template for how I build and approach this. And I think you can do the same thing, and I'm going to use my own business as an example.

Just realize, what I'm about to say is just a framework. You can work within this framework however you want, but that's all it is. One of the reasons I don't have bullet points in these slides is because I really want to encourage you to not take careful notes. I know it sounds weird. Normally, you want that, but this is more of a different way of thinking. And I'm just going to go over how I approach my world. A lot of it will not apply to you. A lot of this is the opposite of what Brian does quite frankly. He's even told you, we do things differently, but it's okay. That's the whole point. You don't want to be anyone else's world. Yours should be different.

You have a world and every world should have doorways that get into it. Doorways that are peppered throughout the internet and offline. Doorways you don't know about. There's word of mouth. Every book I sell on Amazon is a potential doorway. Every time I speak, like right now, this whole platform is a potential doorway into my world.

For anyone who's not already on my list or in my world in some way, this is a potential doorway. You may or may not want to walk through. You will probably experience things a little bit differently than everybody else, and that's the whole point. Every time I get plugged as a useful resource that's a doorway. Every time I get trolled, quite frankly, which happens quite a bit, that's a doorway. I get a lot of leads from my trolls. It's kind of funny. Trolls are not something you should be discouraging. They're unpaid interns, they're great.

There's this mastermind I used to go to and they didn't invite me back for some reason. I don't know why. Maybe they just know my hatred of travel or they're just sick of me, whatever the case may be. But during this mastermind, this was a week ago. I heard from multiple people there. They're like, "Ben, where are you at? Ben, I miss seeing you here. Ben, what's going on? How come you're not here this time?" And I'm like, "I didn't even know they had it this time."

And one person said, "Ben, you don't know me. You have no idea who I am, but I just want to introduce myself. I'm at this mastermind right now, and they just won't stop talking about you. They won't shut up about you, and I just wanted to introduce myself to you." And I thought that was the weirdest email I had gotten in a very long time. I'm not Mr. Social. Nobody would ever accuse me of being the life of the party. Yet here they were asking about my absence.

I was thinking about it where I was putting this together, and I'm thinking this is a perfect example of what happens when you build a world. There are doorways out there you don't even know about and people coming through. I got several opt-ins during that time. I can only assume some of them came from that mastermind. One of those guys I know for a fact came from there and he bought something already.

That's a function of him coming into my world in a way that I've built things. You can't engineer this. This is what, as a direct marketer, I wish I could engineer it. I want to be able to just take everything and say, "Okay, here's how I replicate what I did. Here's what I just saw someone else do. Let me replicate it." I can't engineer this. I can't engineer it with Google, or Facebook, or tracking of any kind. It just happens. It's just a function of people in that room are showing a doorway into my world. Some wanted in, some didn't. And hopefully that makes sense.

For this analogy, since I'm using Narnian vernacular, let say there's a wardrobe. Let's say you find your way in to it via word of mouth, somebody told you something, somebody said something bad about me, who knows, but you were intrigued enough to come into the wardrobe. So, let's say you just came into my email list because I've tried to engineer it so that really the only way to come into my world is through my opt-in, there's no other way to really find me at this point. I like that. I like funneling them in through one way I can keep track of.

And you come inside and you start noticing things look a little bit differently, hopefully, if I've done my job right, than other places in our niche. It's just different in some very obvious ways. In some ways, it probably is not so obvious until you've been on my list for a while. Just from the way I write and sell with emails, the kinds of offers I promote. Like for example, I'm a book guy.

I don't know anyone else who sells $1,000+ print, perfect bound books. Others have been slowly doing it since reading my elBenbo Press book. But I'm first in my niche far as I can tell. So, I've been doing that. I have a whole suite of them now, like 10 or 11 of them. It's just different. It's the way everything looks. The covers look unique. The personality I project and that I put into everything should be unique. The expectations I have of my customers is going to be different. The way I curate customers is going to be a little bit different.

I'm very quick to curate people on or off. I put demands on my customers and would-be customers. I make people jump through certain hoops they're not used to. Probably there are a hundred other little peculiarities that hopefully set my business and my brand apart, and that's the goal. Complete uniqueness. And this is why it's hard to swipe something like this. It's hard to copy it in a way that works because it's got to be unique. It can't really be duplicated or copied.

It would be like trying to copy Tolkien. Tolkien has still the number one-selling books. The Lord of the Rings is still the number one fantasy book series in every bookstore across this country, as far as I know at least, and people were even complaining about this, other writers, fantasy writers. They're like, "Why is this guy still always placed number one?" Because he's the one that sells decades after his stuff came out. Everyone is trying to knock him off, but he built the world everyone is trying to copy, not realizing it's not about copying. It's about building something unique. And that's always been my goal for World-Building, quite frankly, is to make it something unique and on its own.

Now, I want people to come in. This might sound a little strange, but I want it to almost seem magical in the sense that it is different. Maybe it doesn't follow the laws of direct marketing any more than Narnia follows the laws of physics. Okay? I don't have literal talking animals and monsters, but that's the effect I want to give people.

I want it to be this weirdness. Everything stands out. In the Narnia books, you go to Narnia and you see a lamppost in the middle of the woods. You see a talking beaver. You see all this weird stuff. You see Father Christmas being chased by the white witch, and all this weird stuff going on. Weirdness, it's stands out, and that's what I want. It doesn't have to be weird if that isn't your preference or style or way of doing this. But it has to be different, contrasting to everything else your market is seeing.

And if you're reading my emails, and you're clicking to my sites, and you're checking out my mobile apps, and if you're consuming my content and wandering around my world from media to media, it may feel a little cold. So, it's like you go into Narnia, there's ice all over. It's a little cold, right? It's not a warm place. It's not like most marketers where it's a very warm, inviting place. Mine is a little cold. It's strange. I have ways I do things of curating people out and aggressively doing so. And all of that is so I can keep a clean email list as much as possible. I'll have multiple storylines about my business and life going on throughout my emails and throughout my content hopefully giving people options for thinking differently. My whole world is built upon giving options for thinking differently, which is a way of thinking I learned by listening to a comedian, the late comedian, Patrice O'Neal, who was kind of a degenerate in a lot of ways. But the guy was just a wizard at persuasion by giving people options for thinking differently. I built my entire business around that in so many ways. And that's what you see when you come into my world. It's just options for looking at things differently, doing things differently. What I do may not even work for some people. That's fine. It's all about getting people thinking differently and doing things differently— that's the kind of world I wanted to build. Your world will be based around what you like to do, not what I or anyone else likes to do.

So, I'll go around, I'll mock people. I'll mock lazy people. Just this morning in about an hour or so, I have an email going out talking about why I don't cater to newbies. I don't want newbies on my list. I really don't want to deal with them. That will sound strange to some people who are used to being catered to as newbies, and that's okay. But even the newbies will have a place in my world if they understand where their place is. And if they don't, they'll be jettisoned, and I do it all the time.

I'm quick to eject trolls, but I like to use tolls. That's a whole part of my world is I want them in there because they're great email fodder. I make money from trolls. The house I live in now was partially funded by a troll, believe it or not. There was a troll I made something like $30,000 in sales off. And when I had a sale in his honor, when he tried trolling me on Twitter once, and I said, "Well, I'm going to have a sale in this guy's honor. In fact, in my Copy Troll book, I talk about this. And I even titled the chapter, The House That Talib Built, because that's the guy's name—Talib.

And that's my whole point. It's a different way of looking at things. You come into my world, it's just a different place. It may be a little bit of a cold place, quite frankly. It might be a place you don't like, and that's fine. Not everybody is going to like my place.

I may be quick to blacklist somebody because, for example, I blacklist people who leave Email Players and they try to come back. I don't let them come back. And as one person listening to this call and I should apologize to him now. He's like the greatest direct mail guy on the planet and I blocked him. He was like, "Why did you block me?" I said, "Because you canceled." "I've never been on your list." And I checked, and I say, "Oh, yeah…" Sometimes, I make mistakes in this world and that happens. I don't put myself out as this infallible person. It's just a world. It's a different place. It's a smaller world probably. It's a world I want people to want to be in, but I also want to make it clear that if it's not something you like, you should probably leave. There're other places to go.

This is a process I'm constantly going through. And it's something I'm constantly thinking about and adding to. And I can go on and on and on just on this, but I don't think I have that kind of time. So, we will just move on to the next part, and I'm going to give another warning here. I'm going to reiterate what I keep saying about there's no checklist. Obviously, what I just said is not a checklist. It's a way of thinking. It's a state of mind and a way of approaching not just business but life. The whole point is make your world uniquely your own. Your own doorways, your own laws, your own way of doing business, your own way of looking at things, your own way of dealing with customers, your own way of dealing with people.

When people come into your world, it's very obvious. "Oh, this must be a Brian Kurtz email…" Or, "I know I'm talking to a Brian Kurtz Titans Xcelerator person right now, just because of the way this person behaves." That's how it will be. And I've witnessed this, and I witness it in my own business all the time. You can witness it.

I have this rule in my Brand Barbarian book. It's the first rule upon which all the other things I teach in that book rest upon. And that is to always do everything in your power to never look, sound, smell, taste, or feel like any other business, to the extent that's possible.

You're never going to 100% be able to do that. If you really took that to an extreme, you'd probably never make any money because we all do certain things that we know work that other people are doing. But I'm saying at a glance and keep it in context, which all of this, by the way, is kind of like marketing heresy to certain people. People who are given to swiping and copying. Really, think about that. Think about, for example, a company like Agora. I think of like Bill Bonner. And when he started his world out and he started with this completely unique looking ad, sales letter. From what I understand, I may be getting this story wrong, but that international traveling newsletter. It started with that thing that was unique and turned into this gigantic monstrosity that is now its own world.

Now, that's at a huge level. We don't all have to build at that level. But this is what I'm talking about. If you were just to go around copying what other people are doing and saying, "Well, that's what so-and-so is doing. That's what I should be doing." I'm not saying to never do that. I'd never say that. You should always be looking at what's working to some extent but you're only going to get so far doing it. But I think of Martin Goodman, the original owner of Marvel Comics, for example. In the '30s, '40s, and '50s, he became very rich selling comic books, and he was a trend-chaser. Comics were all trends back then, like one-month westerns are selling. The next month, romance comics are selling. The next month, superheroes. And then it goes back to war comics, or horror comics, and on and on and on. And this guy's whole business model was "see what's selling, what's the trend—then flood the market with that product and then wait for it to change and do something else."

And if that doesn't sound suspiciously like the typical internet marketer's mentality you're probably not paying attention. That's what they do. And you can make a lot of money doing it. I'm not saying you can't. It's a very empty, culture-less way to build a company, but you could do it, and people make a lot of money doing it.

Now, enter Stan Lee. Stan Lee was going to quit Marvel, because he got sick of writing these nonsensical stories being told he can only write words with two syllables because they're writing to kids and talking down to the market. Brian mentioned how he and I both have respect for our markets and our lists, and we do. We don't talk down to people. I know in my own copywriting, I break all kinds of these rules like how you supposedly have to write at a 7th grade level. No. I'll put words I don't even understand in there sometimes. I just write. It's a function of communicating. But enter Stan Lee, he says, "Okay, I'm quitting anyway, so I'm going to write one last story, get this out of my system, how I think it should be done." And he writes the Fantastic Four, which blows sales away.

And then, of course, he doesn't quit, and he creates the modern Marvel Comics universe that everybody who watches the movies, at least, is familiar with. That is its own unique universe and world. I mean, you know Marvel when you saw it compared to all the other comic book companies, especially back then. They were all different. He had Thor. He's a god. And then he had Spider-Man on the street level. He had Dr. Strange working magic, and he had The Hulk which is like a modern horror story, and he had the Fantastic Four, which was sci-fi. And then blind lawyer Daredevil. All these completely different, unique personalities, but they were all in the same world. You knew it was a cohesive world. When these characters ran into each other, it made sense, they fit. And that's how you want to build out your offers. And that's how you want your stuff to be. Again, this is just an intro to the subject, but that's one way I want you to think about it.

Now, again, I can't give you checklists, but I can absolutely give you foundations to build upon. It should be obvious right now this is all art and practically zero science. For a lot of direct marketers, they're going to have to think a lot differently. Because this is World-Building. It comes from within.

I've talked about the Narnian world, how C.S. Lewis built that. He didn't have the whole thing figured out beforehand and neither do you have to. Don't let this be more daunting than it has to be. Lewis literally had an image in his head of a faun, the half human, half goat running around the forest with presents in his hand in the snow. That was how he started the entire world that he built. He didn't know what was going to happen after that. He didn't have anything figured out beyond that. He started with a faun in the forest. He was that kind of a writer. And he just kind of went with it. He didn't know.

Tolkien was the same exact way. He didn't know jack about where he was taking The Hobbit beyond I think the sixth chapter. They leave the Misty Mountains and he's like, "now what?" Lord of the Rings was originally just a book about hobbits talking and interacting. There was no Ring or Dark Lord or any of that. The stack of drafts before he figured things out was literally seven feet high. You can read about this in the book Bandersnatch. People look at Tolkien and think, "Wow, he built this world, so methodical!" No, it took him like 50 years to build that because it took him almost 20 years just to get The Fellowship of the Ring right. He went through lots of different versions of it. Used to drive some of his friends in the Inklings crazy how he'd say he was going to do a little tweaking and editing and then just start the thing over from scratch over and over and over.

And that is just how it goes. It was a process of building that world. So it was with C. S. Lewis and with Disney, too. Let's talk about Walt Disney, because obviously, he built a great world. He even called it Disney World and Disneyland. Very literally built worlds. If you ever read his biography by Neal Gabler, *Triumph of the American Imagination*, I highly recommend it. You will see it's obvious, his entire business, everything from his animation studio, how he built the culture there amongst the workers, to his Disneyland and his movies and everything else... was always about getting back to his childhood hometown he missed and that he loved. He just wanted that back. He wanted whatever it was that he lost by not being there. That's what his world was built upon. That's why nobody can copy it. Not Six Flags... nobody could ever copy what he did. They could try, and they do, but they'll never be Disney.

You can say Disney's success is based on their ruthless selling and service and all that. And there's a lot of truth to that. I'm not saying there's not. Vance Morris, he's really big on that. But ultimately, Disney built a world. I think the company peaked, personally, so I don't really like using Disney as an example beyond talking about Walt. But no matter how creative they get at pissing off their customers and destroying the brands they are in charge of, you can always look at what they did in the past to do World-Building.

Apple Computer is the exact same way. Another book I highly recommend for World-Building is called Steve Jobs by Walter Isaacson. And in many ways, Apple's world was built upon Jobs' frustration. He was just frustrated in a lot of ways with IBM and the cold, ruthless, non-craftsmanship way of how the computer world was. His dad taught him when he was a kid to have a sense of craftsmanship. So, this goes back to childhood. I really do think World-Building goes back to our childhood. It's built by something that happens there. Jobs' dad, who was a master craftsman at building cabinets, would instill in young Steve's head this idea of craftsmanship and the importance of it. He would tell young Steve Jobs, "When you're building a cabinet, the back of the cabinet nobody sees should have the exact same high-quality wood and all the attention to detail as the front and places people will see."

And if you look at the early Apple machines, and I think Apple peaked like 10 years ago too for same reasons as Disney, they were the same way. They would put a little screw that was so expensive and high quality and just so well-crafted in the middle of the machine that no customer will ever see. Nobody but an Apple certified technician knows how to open the thing and would ever see it. They put that much attention to detail into it. There's a reason why Apple was known for its culture. It's world and culture are the same thing. Every world has a culture. That's why he would always make fun of Bill Gates. He's like, "Microsoft has no culture. It's soulless."

And they did this thing about 10 or 15 years ago when some scientists measured the brain activity of Apple fans. And then they looked at what happened in their brains when they saw an Apple gadget, and they found out their brains had the same reaction to an Apple gadget as their brains do to their chosen deity they worship. That's the potential power of World-Building. Show me one direct response marketer who does that, who really has that power. I can think of a few, but it's very rare. I mean, that's the effect you want.

I'm not saying you want to be God. But you are building your own alternate reality where you're king, and where you control things. And that's a function of World-Building. You start with one idea. One idea, one offer, one thing you want to do. You start with that something internally, something that's a mixture of your personality, your background, your experience with something. Something that drives you and you're obsessed with or bothered by or really want to see. Maybe it's a wrong you want to right, whatever it is. It's something within you that you build this world upon.

For me, I love giving options for thinking differently. It makes me a better marketer, a better person, a better everything in my life. So, that's what drives me. That doesn't have to drive you. C. S. Lewis, or Apple, or Disney, Fred Rogers' desire to be a good neighbor… everyone is driven by something, and it starts with that internal something. I don't know how to define it. I don't know how to give a checklist for it. It's just there. And you start with that one offer. You start with that one list you build. You start with that next email you send, and you start stacking these things, and the other media you use on top of each other and connecting them.

And soon, you're building out that culture that Steve Jobs talked about. And your competitors look boring and stale and shallow over time. I'm going to argue you have no competitors at this point. They have no soul. They have no culture. They have nothing. Nobody gets excited really by a Windows machine or has Six Flags Great America stickers, orange juice, shirts, etc., around the house. They really don't. I'm not saying people aren't fans of it, but nobody is excited by it like they are Apple stuff or Disney stuff.

I'll even take this back to the comic book industry. I think Marvel has peaked as well too—and it shows in their ticket and comic book sales and loss of customers with what they've been doing. But for now, people will still go see a Marvel movie for characters they've never heard of before. And some of those movies will make a billion dollars. Nobody says, "Oh, I can't wait for the next DC Comics movie to come out!" Nobody does. They might want to see a Batman movie or the Snydercut or something, or Superman, or Wonder Woman. But they don't care about the world that was built as a whole. Huge difference. And that's why the goal is just to build a universe of offers that are unique like that, but that all fit together. Kind of the way that Marvel did it, like Disney has done it, like Apple has done it. So people don't buy just that one offer of yours, but all of them. They aren't even buying the offer, they are buying the world, just like they aren't going to see friggin' Ant-Man or whatever—they are seeing another "Marvel" movie.

You can look at an Apple gadget, an Apple computer, an Apple phone. And I'm not even an Apple fanboy, so I don't even have an iPhone, but I can look at Apple stuff and say, "That's Apple. That's Apple's world." I know when I'm talking to an Apple fanboy, quite frankly. They can't help themselves. That's because Apple did such a great job building a world. Or at least Steve Jobs did, not so much anymore in my opinion. And I think that's important to realize. Look at how these worlds were built, not how a bunch of stuffed suits are managing—or mismanaging—them now.

As far as a framework goes, and again, I have to keep saying, I wish there was a checklist, but there's not. The good news is you're already probably doing most of this. Most of the nuts-and-bolts stuff, you already got. The fact you're at this mastermind, you already got the nuts-and-bolts stuff. You know how to market. You know how to sell. You know how to write copy. And if not, you know how to hire and outsource what you need to. That's the hard part. That takes, at least, skill, if not talent. It takes something you have to learn. World-Building simply takes patience.

You just have to change the way you think about things. You're no longer a seller of products or services, you are something else now. You're king and emperor of your own world. I mean, that's the only way I can put it. I had a discussion with Ken McCarthy a few months ago. He wasn't talking about World-Building, but he said this as a function of copywriting—that if you can build this alternate reality, which is just World-Building, he goes, "A lot of the selling is already done for you." And in order to do this, in order to really build a world, and there's no way around this, you have to stop thinking transaction or selling the transaction. Transactions are important. They have to be done. Every email I send out, I go for a sale or transaction. I'm not saying to not sell. You'll never hear me talk about nurture sequences, for example, on email. I don't believe in it. I sell, I don't nurture or pretend I have nothing to sell. But I am also selling me. You have to sell you first. You are the first sale. The relationship is the first sale. You can't even do it by swiping. It has to come from within you. Everything comes and is driven by that. Every email you write, every piece of copy you write, every product you create, every video you make, every customer service activity you do is driven by whatever that thing is internally that is building your world, and that's selling you before you sell anything else.

Every media you use is no longer a media. It's its own little society within your world. So, if you have a social media audience, that's a society within your world. If you have an email list, that's a society in your world. If you have mobile app followers, like I do, it's a society. If you have a direct mail list, if you have a fax list for those who still have those, which I still think there's value in that, that's a society. Some of these people may overlap. Some may not. It doesn't matter. It's going to be obvious to all of them whose world they're in and that's yours.

Everything now is a character in your world. Every offer you create is its own flesh-and-blood character. As real as a friend or neighbor. Every employee you have is a character in your world. Every business partner is a character. Every affiliate, every vendor, everyone you come in contact with is now a citizen, character whatever you want to call it in your world.

They may do things that are completely out of character for them. They may do weird things. When you start looking at things like this, you'll start seeing happy accidents. And when you start applying this way of thinking of making everything a little bit different, so it doesn't look, sound, feel, touch, or smell like anything else, you can apply it to your titles.

How many titles just sound like everyone else's titles? I'm not saying it never works. Because you can take something that works in one market and apply it to another. I'm not saying that never works. But what I'm saying is you should think bigger than that. And every product should have its own look and feel, but still be you, and still be something recognized by your audience as belonging in your world. And it has its own personality. Every offer should have its own personality, which will be an extension in some way of your personality.

I can tell you right now, my favorite way of doing this is email. I call myself an email supremacist partly as a joke. Because for some reason, the word triggers some people, but also because it's true. I think it's the supreme platform for selling above all others. And if you want the tactical advice here, use daily email. Send a minimum of one email per day to continuously build your world. It creates proximity and familiarity to you and to your world.

It's also a function of leadership. I don't see how anybody can lead their market if they're not constantly in touch with their market. In order to build a world people want to be in and don't want to leave, you have to be a leader. You have to be someone where you set the trends. And it's all based on what they want and what's good for them, but it may not be things they're necessarily asking for.

I can tell you right now, there's not a single book of mine that I charge up anywhere from $200 to over $1,000 that anybody is asking for. Even the cheap ones, like my Villains books, nobody ever said, "Ben, I want a book teaching persuasion and how to have charisma using villains as an example." Nobody asked for that. It would be silly. Nobody would even think to ask for that. But because I have a daily dialogue with my list, I knew they'd want it and benefit from it. Nobody has ever asked me to write a book about branding, either. And yet, my Brand Barbarian is the second highest book in sales I have. Nobody asked me to write a book about list building. I'm probably the worst list builder in the world. I'm like the last person to ask about list building. I admit this on the sales letter. I am the last person anybody should learn list building from, because I'm a referral guy. And yet, people wanted me to teach it. They kept asking me about the subject because I have that daily contact, so I knew it'd sell and benefit people before even creating it.

Now, I'm going to give an example that I hope will make sense. In Wing

Chun Kung Fu we have this thing called chi sau. It's not sparring, but you're in contact with your partner, and you're kind of trying to find an opening in their defense, and they're trying to do the same to you. And it's very much a feeling thing. You're trying to feel and interpret what they're going to do before they do it.

And so, take these old old kung fu masters who look like they're moving really fast. They look quick. But really, they're as slow as any old man. They simply feel what the other person is going to do before the other person does it. As sifu says, "it's not how fast you are, it's how quickly you get there." And it looks like they're fast, but they're really just interpreting what the other person is going to do, so they get there quicker. That's what daily email will do. It's like chi sau with your list. And I've been doing this in business and while building my world for so long now I don't worry about what my next offer is going to be.

I didn't even want to do a book about social media, but I knew that the demand was there. In fact, I didn't want to create a social media platform, but the demand was there because I kept hearing from people because of the feedback they give me as a result of always being in contact with them. Of constantly feeling and interpreting what they want before they even think to ask for it. And it's not often even directly asked for. It's just something they say, a question they ask, a way they describe their problems and pains and desires. Or it could be they ask about what others are doing, drop names, talk about other offers… it's something you interpret and feel. And in order to build a world, I really believe you have to do it this way. You have to be in some kind of contact with them daily, and preferably and especially with email.

If for no other reason because you want to position yourself as a leader and not just an expert. Because people listen to experts, but they follow leaders, and they'll more eagerly and passionately come into the world of a leader over a mere expert. Experts are a dime a dozen now, especially nowadays where anyone can put up a book on Amazon or write an article or make a YouTube video. But a leader, a true leader… people will seek out. They will climb to the top of the mountain to seek the guidance of a leader—and to enter a leader's world. And that's what you ultimately want.

I don't have anything against surveys and asking what people want. I'm not saying to never do that. Sometimes it's a good idea. But ultimately, it's about leading. And I talk about Steve Jobs a lot because he was the master at that. Did anybody ask for any of the things he did? Not really. There's a story about the Macintosh, when they first launched it, and it was a huge success. This reporter from *Popular Science* says, "Wow, this was a huge hit. What kind of market research did you do?" And Steve goes, "I didn't do any market research. Did Alexander Graham Bell do market research before he invented the telephone?" To him, it was just so obvious. This is what the market wanted and he was leading them to it. He brought them into his world. So, it's a process of discovery. And it's never going to end. If you do it right, it's never going to end. It's going to be something you do forever.

Think of it in terms of this: Don't build businesses, build worlds. It's a different way of thinking. Businesses can be boarded up. A business can be canceled by the state. My business partner in software literally had this happen to him on a small scale. The State of Florida lost his business in their systems. His business ceased to exist for 24 hours. He was panicking, because he has all these merchant accounts, everything around this one entity. It could be taken away. It could be canceled by something, by a platform or a bureaucrat or a judge or whatever.

A business can be beaten by competition. A business has competition. I would argue a world doesn't. Whatever business you're in, There're lots of people in your business, but there's only one you, which means there's only going to be one world like yours that you build, especially if you follow what we're talking about here. There are a lot of "email guys" out there. But there's only one me, only one world like mine, only one of us thinking on this level, quite frankly.

When you really understand World-Building, you understand that other businesses or competitors aren't really the problem. You don't have competition. I don't think Brian has competition. I don't really have competition. I've built a world that transcends competition, and I couldn't care less what anyone else is doing, or are saying, or scheming up. I'm too busy over here in my world, serving my customers, and cultivating a world where they love being inside and don't want to leave, and many of them don't even look at what anyone else is selling or doing any more than the children in the Narnia movies cared what was going on in Middle-Earth or the real world.

The only thing that is your "competitor" at this point if you start building worlds and not just a business is everything that takes people out of your world. So, it could be entertainment. It could be real life. It could be problems. Somebody died. That's going to take people out of your world, at least temporarily at times. It could be current events. It could be a lot of things.

If you have Netflix, watch The Social Dilemma. You'll see that they're master world builders, but not in a good way. You could say the same about Google. There's another documentary on Amazon Prime called *The Creepy Line*, and you'll find out that they're great at building worlds and keeping you in there, but it's almost not by your choice. You want to do the opposite. You want to build a business that people want to be in. They hear about it. They come into it. They don't want to leave. And it is a choice, without you having to play games or deceive anyone.

I'll take you back to the Narnia stories. If you ever read the books or watched the movies, they went to Narnia. When they're in Narnia, which happens during World War II when London is being bombed, they're in this other world. Do you think they give a crap about World War II? Do you think they care who's president? Or Churchill's latest speech? Do they care about what's going on? No, they don't care. They were brought into a different world that was fascinating and exciting. A world they didn't want to leave.

When they did leave and they got ejected, and in fact, they forgot about the real world for 15 years in the first book. Fifteen years ago by where they become kings and queens. They forget it. The book described it as like they remembered it like someone remembers a dream. That's World-Building done right. And then when they left that world, all they could talk about was how they wished they could get back to that world. That's the effect you want. If someone leaves your world, they're like, "Shoot, I need to get back!"

When I eject somebody from my world like trolls or reply guys, it's not uncommon for them to get bitter about it and get butt hurt about it and complain about it, which is not unlike the Narnia stories, where the character Susan was not allowed to come back. And instead of going out with dignity, She's like, "Well, yeah, we used to play games. You kids need to grow up now." Like it never happened and as if she didn't miss it and tried to pretend it never even existed. Such was her bitterness. And people will become bitter if you kick them out because they are disrespectful or trolling or whatever, and that's how you know you're doing it right.

To sum all this up, World-Building means you become the place people want to be. They don't want to leave. You become the distraction. Your world becomes their entertainment. Your world is their current events. Your world, and you are their guy, their advocate, their protector, like Aslan. If you want to use Narnia as the analogy, that's you. And in order to get them in your world like that, you have to build a world first. And I hope this has given you guys some fodder for that. And of course, if you want to enter my world, if you're not in there, it's at BenSettle.com. And that's all I got on that, Brian.

BRIAN KURTZ: That was awesome, Ben. The big aha moment came really early for me when you said there's no checklist. So, I assume that was your excuse to not have a detailed PowerPoint. Actually, just the opposite, because there really is no blueprint for this, except your imagination, how you're thinking big about your world. And I got a lot out of it. I took some notes.

Women-Building 101

Training from the prestigious Profit Pirates coaching program.
www.EmailPlayers.com/pirates

BEN SETTLE: Put the phone down.

STEFANIA: Oh, you did start recording.

BEN SETTLE: All right. I'm not going to yell at you, Stefania, because I actually need you on my side for this one.

STEFANIA: Only this one? I didn't realize you were recording. You said before we started...

BEN SETTLE: It's okay. All right? I don't want to hear any more about this. I rule these conversations with an iron fist. All right. That means be quiet when I say be quiet.

STEFANIA: Okay, Doctor Doom!

BEN SETTLE: Now I got this question from an Email Players subscriber who will not be named.

STEFANIA: Do I know them?

BEN SETTLE: I don't think you do.

STEFANIA: Okay.

BEN SETTLE: I'm not naming him because this question was asked in confidence. The only reason I have you here is because I think your perspective might possibly be useful.

STEFANIA: Maybe? Just a little bit?

BEN SETTLE: Well, it depends on what you say.

STEFANIA: Okay.

BEN SETTLE: So context, he's replying to the March [2022] *Email Player 's* issue where I talked about the parallels between relationships, and dating, and marketing. So even though his question is not directly about marketing, copywriting, business, persuasion, anything like that, it has everything to do with it, but not on the surface. I'm just saying this mostly for the listener. I know you get it because you've been well trained by me. Or actually tamed. Tamed with a whip and a chair.

STEFANIA: Or well indoctrinated.

BEN SETTLE: Well indoctrinated, yes. Exactly. So that's the context. He says, "So I've been rereading that issue a few times recently, as you recommend." Absolutely. I told people to read it multiple times. There's way too much in there just to do it once.

STEFANIA: I know, you yell at me if I'm not reading it.

BEN SETTLE: Absolutely. In fact, I think that issue is still in its envelope. Maybe it's better this way. I don't know. He continued, "…for use in both business, which I'm getting some great ideas for, and in my personal life, where I feel some fear and some old habits. I used to have some low value and weak habits and I've spent the last few years correcting. I'm recently in a new relationship built on the right foundations." Well, that remains to be seen.

STEFANIA: Right. And also makes me wonder what the wrong foundation was in the other ones.

BEN SETTLE: First of all, let me be very clear here. I respect this guy and his decision. I really do because this is the kind of stuff I used to think about 20 years ago, in the 90s.

STEFANIA: You mean when I was in middle school?

BEN SETTLE: When you were in middle school. I used to think this stuff too. So here's my point. There'll be no ridiculing of him or any of that. Nothing we're about to say, none of this, it's not mocking, but we may have some fun with him. That's all I'm saying. And my whole thought is, he would not be asking this question if he was secure in his relationship now.

STEFANIA: Well, that's why he says, "Well, this relationship with the right foundation." Suggests…

BEN SETTLE: I don't think there's a right foundation. I think my friend here is already worried about something and maybe he doesn't need to be. But like he said, past habits, right? That's just how you think. All right. You're going to love the rest of this question, by the way.

STEFANIA: Oh, boy.

BEN SETTLE: He goes, "But I'm afraid of running into the future by falling back in old bad habits from being a low value, nice guy." Something that Stefania does not suffer from having to deal with, let me tell you. He continues, "You mention your 'hobbit style life.'"

STEFANIA: Why is it in quotes?

BEN SETTLE: Because he literally put...

STEFANIA: I know, but it is a hobbit...

BEN SETTLE: It's literally in quotes.

STEFANIA: I know, but it's not a suggestion. It is.

BEN SETTLE: He says, "You mentioned your hobbit style life, but also how you should be high status and pull her into your world and invite her along to things you are already going to enjoy." Now, we're not done. And by the way, I do have a hobbit lifestyle.

STEFANIA: I know.

BEN SETTLE: I am a Baggins, not a... Hold on. You were a Took before you met me.

STEFANIA: Yes. I'm still a Took.

BEN SETTLE: I was a Baggins. The only reason you know me is because I was reluctantly pulled out of my hobbit hole, taken to New York for the Good Cop, Bad Cop, Insane Cop thing, thanks to Ryan Lee and Dan Meredith. And I didn't want to go.

STEFANIA: Did you not want to go?

BEN SETTLE: I wanted to do an event with them. But I didn't want to go to fricking New York.

STEFANIA: And you weren't even really in New York proper, you were in Westchester.

BEN SETTLE: That is as close to New York as I like to get. He asks, "How exactly do you portray status and high value and with that kind of lifestyle?" In other words, he's saying Bilbo Baggins is a dork. How the hell can you be cool to any woman? Is what he's saying.

STEFANIA: Well, you live like a retiree.

BEN SETTLE: We're going to get to all this. Does that count as sitting around with a movie? Why is that funny, Stefania? Please explain to the class why that's funny.

STEFANIA: Because you literally have Top Gun paused right now.

BEN SETTLE: The first Top Gun, in anticipation for the second one.

STEFANIA: Right. And by the way, we didn't realize until today that this is now Willis 'new favorite.

BEN SETTLE: My genes have passed very nicely to Willis. Let's put it that way.

STEFANIA: I've never seen him so excited and so vocal.

BEN SETTLE: He was screaming at the TV. So, to answer this question, yes. In this house, watching movies, and especially movies we watch over and over and over until Stefania is so bored by the movies, She's on her phone the whole time, is absolutely cool.

STEFANIA: But you know how I watch movies. I'm doing other things, but I'm still watching it.

BEN SETTLE: I know. I'm giving him context here. Hold on. We're not done. Put the phone away.

STEFANIA: I'm just looking...

BEN SETTLE: Listen, Willis is not going to get kidnapped by somebody right now.

STEFANIA: Well, I don't know. Maybe.

BEN SETTLE: He won't.

STEFANIA: You're so high value. Maybe.

BEN SETTLE: My high value does make him a high target risk.

STEFANIA: If we were in Latin America.

BEN SETTLE: If we were in Mexico, he 'd already have been kidnapped. Yes, I know that.

STEFANIA: Yeah, multiple times.

BEN SETTLE: Okay. So hold on though, this is the last part. He asks, "And how do you get her to invest more energy and money into you?" Well, first of all, Stefania...

STEFANIA: No, in the beginning I bought my own plane tickets to come here.

BEN SETTLE: Your friend was very mad. "Doesn't he send for you???" Hell no, I don't send for her.

STEFANIA: I'm like, "No, I bought my own plane ticket."

BEN SETTLE: He finishes off the question, "While at the same time, having to portray that you have the power." Now I think this is a great question, by the way. I love this question. And we're going to spend a lot of time dissecting this question and praising me at the same time. Okay. Very important. Which is why you're here. I could have answered this myself. In fact, that hour that I spend before kung fu lessons, where I'm just kind of parked because I like to go early everywhere because I'm a Baggins.

STEFANIA: You're not five minutes earlier, you're at least 50 minutes earlier.

BEN SETTLE: I was over an hour early and I could have recorded an answer to this. Instead, I thought, this is a perfect opportunity to pull Stefania into my world once again.

STEFANIA: Like Hades pulling down... Is it Persephone?

BEN SETTLE: I was thinking more like a tractor beam pulling the Millennium Falcon into the Death Star. Okay. So let's start from this, so my Hobbit lifestyle. It should not be in quotes, by the way. Hold on. So the Hobbit lifestyle, explain what you were before you met me because it'll make a lot more sense. You were a club-hopping Manhattanite.

STEFANIA: Not club-hopping, but I was definitely a bar-hopping Manhattanite, for sure. I used to go out almost every day.

BEN SETTLE: And you were in law school.

STEFANIA: I was in law school. Well, before law school I used to go out a lot, and then even during law school, I used to go out a lot.

BEN SETTLE: And this is in Manhattan.

STEFANIA: This is in Manhattan.

BEN SETTLE: New York.

STEFANIA: So this is where the weekend starts on Thursday night. I used to go out after class, which class let out at 10, so that should tell you how late it would be. And I would sleep for three hours and go to work the next day. And then on Saturdays, you go and do something during the day or you go meet up with somebody, do something at night. And then on Sunday, you have hangover brunch. And then you kind of just recuperate so you can start all this shit all over again on Monday. I was always out of the house. I hated being home and I was always out.

BEN SETTLE: And you had some unsavory friends.

STEFANIA: I did. Who were...

BEN SETTLE: People you are now ashamed of.

STEFANIA: Yeah. They were... I wouldn't say I was a lush. But I hung out with a lot of lushes. And yeah, they were...

BEN SETTLE: Stefania, hold on. Now, you wanted to come visit me in Bandon, which is not much different than where I'm at now, just an hour south, but the same ocean...

STEFANIA: Actually, there was more of a nightlife in Bandon than there is here.

BEN SETTLE: Which isn't saying much.

STEFANIA: The nightlife is two bars.

BEN SETTLE: And what did I do when you wanted to come out? What did I keep telling you?

STEFANIA: You told me that I would hate it. That I would not want to be there. That I shouldn't come because there's no brunch, which by the way was a lie. There is brunch.

BEN SETTLE: Well, yeah. And it was right at Lord Bennett's a block away.

STEFANIA: Yeah within walking distance so you lied.

BEN SETTLE: It wasn't your kind of brunch.

STEFANIA: No, it wasn't. No. No it wasn't the same thing. And you told me that I would be bored out of my mind. That's actually verbatim when you said I'd be bored out of my mind and I'd hate it.

BEN SETTLE: Because I had other chicks I wanted to date and I didn't want you cramping my style.

STEFANIA: Oh really?

BEN SETTLE: But you fought your way through. All right. Now, when you came out to visit me and you saw my hobbit lifestyle, and you were not... Let's be very clear, it was the antithesis of everything you've ever known.

STEFANIA: You were the antithesis of everything that I've ever known.

BEN SETTLE: It was unheard of you'd even go to a place like that unless it was on vacation or something.

STEFANIA: The last time I ever went to anywhere remotely like Bandon was going to Florida with my parents when I was in middle school. My vacation I went to grand canyon with my friends and that's not the same thing.

BEN SETTLE: And what happened, Stefania, after the first time you visited me? What did you do in the plane when you had to leave?

STEFANIA: I cried.

BEN SETTLE: And why did you cry?

STEFANIA: Because I didn't want to go home.

BEN SETTLE: Okay so this is my point.

STEFANIA: I cried.

BEN SETTLE: This is my point because he's asking about bringing a woman into your world. Right?

STEFANIA: Right.

BEN SETTLE: And he's worried about, well, do I have to, how do he put it here—"How do I get her to invest more time and energy? How do I show that I'm exciting and all that? How do I portray status?" Did I have to do any of that with you? Or did I just bring you into my world? And I let you decide if it was for you or not. And by the way, let be very clear, you were absolutely on probation at that time.

STEFANIA: Yeah, I was.

BEN SETTLE: All right.

STEFANIA: I remember when we walked to your office and I need to get something, I don't know what it was. And you ran into somebody that you knew and you basically shoved me into the street.

BEN SETTLE: Yes I did.

STEFANIA: And you were like, "I don't know her."

BEN SETTLE: Absolutely. Absolutely.

STEFANIA: And I was standing really close. I think I was even holding your hand or something.

BEN SETTLE: And I threw your hand out of mine because I may have other plans. At that stage of the relationship you had not earned your spot. You were an intern. You were not even a temp or so much as on the payroll. And you sure as hell were not a partner in the firm. Okay? You were a lowly intern in the mail room.

STEFANIA: I was going to say, not even the mail clerk.

BEN SETTLE: And I was still taking applications for people who wanted to be in my world. Now that said, I found you, I tamed you. Okay? You came into my world.

STEFANIA: I know.

BEN SETTLE: And you never wanted to leave.

STEFANIA: No, I don't to this day.

BEN SETTLE: Okay. This is important because obviously I had dated many women before you.

STEFANIA: Harrumph.

BEN SETTLE: And some of them liked my world. Some even didn't want to leave the world either. And I had to kind of pry them out a little bit. "Shoo. Go." Some left on their own, didn't want to come back, while others left and now wish they'd stayed. And that is just how it goes and how it should be.

STEFANIA: Your world is very comfortable.

BEN SETTLE: My world, and I warned you this, did I not? I said, women tend to gain a little weight in my world because I'm a hobbit.

STEFANIA: Because all we did...

BEN SETTLE: Good food, my warm hearth, my beach, my dog… and my point is I built a world that I like to be in. Now, this brings up something else we were talking about related to Top Gun. This is why it's very important because if I say this stuff without you here, nobody believes me. It sounds like I'm one of these losers on Facebook saying "I have no fucks to give!" right?

STEFANIA: Yeah. Zero fucks given.

BEN SETTLE: I lose track of all these stupid things. All right. And "AF" and all that dorky vernacular. All right. So we were watching Top Gun and I said, "you know who reminds me of Tony Scott, the director?" He's a very stylistic director, Tony Scott.

STEFANIA: This is specific style.

BEN SETTLE: It's very stylish. Like the little goofy guys at the beginning, on the aircraft carrier dancing. They're so excited to be doing their job.

STEFANIA: Yeah.

BEN SETTLE: And I said, "you know who reminds me of Ton Scott? Michael Bay." And you said, what?

STEFANIA: That you're the Michael Bay of email.

BEN SETTLE: Which some people say, "Ben, do you really want to claim that title?" Well, I'm not claiming anything.

STEFANIA: He's a billionaire. Why wouldn't I?

BEN SETTLE: I'm not claiming any titles, but there was a reason why you said that.

STEFANIA: Right. Because between Michael Bay and Tony Scott, they both direct and create films with shit they find cool.

BEN SETTLE: What they think is cool. They don't care what anyone else thinks.

STEFANIA: Right. And even so Michael Bay… I went to performing art school where you had the film conservatory and everything. And so if I even mentioned his name out loud, people would be like.

BEN SETTLE: He was the Donald Trump of performing arts.

STEFANIA: Right. But meanwhile his films literally make billions of dollars.

BEN SETTLE: The ones that everybody in the performing arts schools hate make a lot of money.

STEFANIA: Right. They make a lot of money because the thing is, he's tapping into something just like what red-blooded American guys think is cool, which is explosions, chicks with big boobs and just cool shit, right? Cars that turn into machines. How is that not cool? So he just does things...

BEN SETTLE: Cars that turn into robots.

STEFANIA: True.

BEN SETTLE: They're already machines Stefania. Hold on. I have to, even five years later, I have to correct you and lead you

STEFANIA: I wasn't really that into Transformers.

BEN SETTLE: I have to lead you. It's okay. I have to lead you.

STEFANIA: I know.

BEN SETTLE: It is my job.

STEFANIA: I only saw a few of the cartoons.

BEN SETTLE: So first of all, what you're making is a very good point for business and for a man. By the way, nothing we're talking about is going to help a woman. Let's just be very clear about that.

STEFANIA: You don't think so?

BEN SETTLE: No. I don't think any of this will help a woman.

STEFANIA: It just helps get women. I'm sorry.

BEN SETTLE: No, no. Help a woman. It will not help a woman.

STEFANIA: Well, I think to some extent...

BEN SETTLE: Hold on, are you contradicting me?

STEFANIA: No. I'm just saying that the part of doing things that you find cool, the problem is though for women and I know some people are going to be like, isn't true, but whatever. I don't care.

BEN SETTLE: Nobody cares what women think anyways. Don't worry about it.

STEFANIA: Women—we tend to be really focused. Even you can go into beauty standards, whether it's fashion, we're very outwardly focused of what people think or perceive of us based on what we wear...

BEN SETTLE: And this is why you are more concerned with what a woman thinks of how you dress than the guy that you like. Now, not you personally, you actually defy that. You actually crave my opinion on what to wear. You yell at me if I don't give you my opinion. What did you say to me?

STEFANIA: I told you if there's something that I'm wearing that you don't like, tell me about it.

BEN SETTLE: You want me to curate your...

STEFANIA: Oh yeah. Yeah, yeah.

BEN SETTLE: This is why you have to be here saying this. If I say it, nobody believes me, sounds like I'm lying.

STEFANIA: I told you, I want your help with curating my outfits.

BEN SETTLE: Why is that, Stefania?

STEFANIA: You have a very specific style. If I threw all your clothes in the air and just grab randomly, they'll all match. And I don't have that ability. Because everything is all in the same color palette, you could just wear whatever or even go into your closet blindly and start pulling stuff out. They'll all coordinate together.

BEN SETTLE: Now, on your New York dates…

STEFANIA: Yes.

BEN SETTLE: The guys in New York, and I'm talking about the guys, not the feminine guys, the actual guys. With more testosterone than estrogen.

STEFANIA: Which are very far and few in between.

BEN SETTLE: The point is, there's something about the way I do things you like. Now what I do is not exciting to anyone else. But it's exciting to you.

STEFANIA: It is.

BEN SETTLE: Because you were drawn into my world. Liked what you saw, I cannot get rid of you if I wanted to. That's how much you liked it. And I don't have to worry about this stuff what he's saying here, about getting you to invest more energy and money trying...

STEFANIA: It's not a status.

BEN SETTLE: I don't have to portray power and status. It's all built-in.

STEFANIA: So, going back to the clothes thing, and I know this is maybe more of a girl thing than a guy thing, but I think that depending on who you're talking to. Guys are like, "oh, you have to wear a Rolex. You have to wear these shoes or whatever, these Balenciaga."

BEN SETTLE: I don't think about any of that stuff.

STEFANIA: No, you have your very specific style but it suits you. It looks good on you.

BEN SETTLE: I play my game.

STEFANIA: Right. You wear clothes that are really well fitted for you. That's number one, you wear things that are really well fitted for you and they're the colors that compliment you, and they're things that you like to wear all the time. So, you look comfortable and there is something about people, where they are more attractive when they're wearing something they're comfortable in versus they're just wearing something that's very obviously not meant for them. So, you just wear cool.

BEN SETTLE: To you it's cool, but to your friends in New York, they would think I was the biggest dork in the world.

STEFANIA: Right. But meanwhile...

BEN SETTLE: But I wouldn't be caring what those hoochies think so it doesn't matter.

STEFANIA: But you have hipsters wearing purposefully hard hat stuff. Meanwhile, they've never seen a power tool in their life. So you have people who are trying to do this whole lumberjack thing, they're trying to be down to earth but they're wearing super expensive stuff. Meanwhile, you are wearing down-to-earth stuff but it's all these other criteria which is like you wear jeans that fit you in a very specific way. You wear boots that fit you in a very specific way. You wear your leather jackets that fit you in a very specific way. And all of it is cool because it's the stuff that you like.

BEN SETTLE: It's cool.

STEFANIA: It's very obvious it's the things that you like.

BEN SETTLE: It's cool to me. And it's cool to the select women who want to be in my world. It's not cool to everyone or to all women.

STEFANIA: No, it's not.

BEN SETTLE: Right. And that's my whole point. What I'm trying to say for him, he has to just build his world and not worry about trying to impress people, trying to have power and status and all that. None of that matters. That's all posturing. That's for people with very little minds, not that he has one. I know where he is coming from. I'm not making fun of him, but what I'm saying is that's for people where the consequences mean nothing. You got to play your game.

STEFANIA: But you have to know what your game is though. We've had this conversation in another...

BEN SETTLE: Well, that was the next issue of the Email Players—the April 2022 issue. Although it wasn't talking about this, it was talking about business. But the principle applies.

STEFANIA: And We've talked about this before and most people don't know what they like, or they don't know what their game is. Their idea of what their game is is what other people are telling them what their game is. Which it could be anything. It could be well, cool people or people of this certain status wear these things, this is an example. Or they watch these movies. Or they're, like I said, at my old college it's like nobody of any taste likes Michael Bay.

BEN SETTLE: Meanwhile I have the first two Transformers movies and The Rock on my Amazon Prime.

STEFANIA: You have to watch art house if you are in that crowd. I mean, there's some good art house movies but really no one sits down and actually genuinely enjoys it as a—

BEN SETTLE: If a woman really liked that, she would be miserable in my world. And that's okay. And I would say, she needs to go find another world.

STEFANIA: Right. So, you self select them out if they... you don't try to shoehorn.

BEN SETTLE: You got to curate it.

STEFANIA: Right. And you also don't shoehorn other people's tastes into yours. And also you don't, like if I didn't like it you'd be like, "Okay, well there's the door."

BEN SETTLE: There are four doors to the outside in this house. Go pick one. And don't let it hit you in the ass on the way out. With you I was trying to get you to complain. And it's not a trick. I am in curation mode at that point. I got to test this woman to see if She's going to last. Because as you know, I've had certain exes do stupid things like try to take me to hibachi restaurants.

STEFANIA: Why would they do that?

BEN SETTLE: Because they're not thinking.

STEFANIA: You went to a hibachi restaurant, it's like one of the circles of hell for you, I don't understand why anyone…

BEN SETTLE: Oh, it was, trust me.

STEFANIA: Why would you?

BEN SETTLE: I'm just glad nobody else was at the table. I was getting sick of the chef. Wanted to say, "just give me the food. Quit talking."

STEFANIA: You didn't want the beating heartbeat.

BEN SETTLE: I didn't want the guy talking.

STEFANIA: Rice or whatever.

BEN SETTLE: I didn't want the guy talking.

STEFANIA: Flaming onions.

BEN SETTLE: He just kept talking and yapping. I'm like, "just shut up and feed me."

STEFANIA: You didn't want to sit in a communal table.

BEN SETTLE: Let me tell you, I got stuck at one of the, what was it? Is it called tapis?

STEFANIA: Tapas.

BEN SETTLE: Oh, I'm sorry. *Tapas*. Okay. So, I was speaking at this event, the Health Profits Summit. We all went to this tapas.

STEFANIA: People who liked hibachi.

BEN SETTLE: With people and everyone there, I mean, everybody's so close and they're all talking. I can see the spit coming out of their mouths when they're talking into the food and I'm holding my plate up like this to my face. Guarding it from all these people.

STEFANIA: Most of tapas you're supposed to share the food.

BEN SETTLE: I don't share.

STEFANIA: I know you don't.

BEN SETTLE: I don't share with you. And I sure won't share with a bunch of idiot strangers looking at my plate.

STEFANIA: I know.

BEN SETTLE: Here's my point. That's my way. Right?

STEFANIA: You don't share.

BEN SETTLE: Now, there was a time you were not all that okay with that. Now you're in my world and I think you understand why I'm like that.

STEFANIA: Well, it's also...

BEN SETTLE: You understand a lot of, I'm trying to get this out to you Stefania.

STEFANIA: No.

BEN SETTLE: You are more, I'm not going to say you're more right wing, because you're about equal with me now.

STEFANIA: Yeah.

BEN SETTLE: However, you're more intense about your right wing ways since Willis has been born. And second of all, you're almost as reclusive as me now.

STEFANIA: I know you've almost...

BEN SETTLE: Your patience with people is at an all time low. You have become part of my world. I've assimilated you into the elBenborg collective.

STEFANIA: Well, I was...

BEN SETTLE: I did not join your world. I did not go to New York to hang. All I wanted to do is get the hell out of New York the couple times I was there.

STEFANIA: So one thing I'll say that New Yorkers don't like other people. For such a huge city we hate everyone.

BEN SETTLE: It's one of the only things I agree with.

STEFANIA: But you've only amplified that. I really can't stand anybody, but I'm really nice. Don't get me wrong. But when I'm... I have the worst road rage now.

BEN SETTLE: I have tell you that you can't just honk at these boomers. You can give them a heart attack.

STEFANIA: I know. And it's like my hands twitch because I wanted to yell at people.

BEN SETTLE: And understand, listen to this. There is no rush hour in Gold Beach. No hurry in Curry.

STEFANIA: I know. There isn't. And it makes me wonder how did I drive in Manhattan? How did I do that? I mean, I did it very sparingly. I did it like in driver's ed. Right? But how did I not have an aneurism in the back of a cab? I don't know.

BEN SETTLE: Well, I definitely had an aneurism in the back of the Ubers. I'm not going to go into that. But here's the point. I built a world that was built around me first. And I invited you to come take a peek and you poked your head inside and you said, "oh, this looks interesting..." And then you timidly put a foot in there and you're like, "oh, that's kind of cool..." And you looked around, and it was like Narnia. Right? You came through the wardrobe.

STEFANIA: And actually Nicole called it Narnia.

BEN SETTLE: Yes. Nicole used to call it Narnia for you because she talked to you and she noticed how happy you were when you were at my house versus in New York.

STEFANIA: Oh God. I used to cry all the time.

BEN SETTLE: Absolutely.

STEFANIA: I was so depressed.

BEN SETTLE: And you walked into the wardrobe off the plane and into my world and you saw it is kind of cold in here. Ben's kind of a cold guy. I was the white witch.

STEFANIA: The gringo warlock.

BEN SETTLE: The gringo warlock. Instead of that dwarf, I had Zoe, I gave you some Turkish delight and you were like, "huh? This is pretty good. Where can I get more?" And I said, "no, you have to leave." And then I kicked you out just like the white witch sent Edmund away. I sent you away and you couldn't stop thinking about coming back to my house—to my world.

STEFANIA: I came back two weeks later.

BEN SETTLE: You would come back as often as possible. And if I said, I want you out there...

STEFANIA: Well you didn't say it.

BEN SETTLE: I didn't say it like that. I'm much nicer about it now than I was then.

STEFANIA: I know you missed me when you start arguing with me.

BEN SETTLE: And guess what? Five years and a baby later, here you are. Because I built a world and this is the whole point. This might sound like I'm kind of self-propping and I am a little bit. But the reality is this, I built a world based on what I think is cool. I lived my life how I want to live it. I had my goals, they had nothing to do with you, and you liked watching me achieve one goal after another. You watched me write the last of my books, basically you watched my entire business double, right? You've watched this and you watch me even now. But all those things I do and am striving for are independent of you. If you came or gone it wouldn't matter, I'd still do this. This world would still be here, there'd just be a different Latina sitting here I'd have to replace you with if you left.

STEFANIA: It makes me want to support you.

BEN SETTLE: And this is why this talk will do women no good.

STEFANIA: No.

BEN SETTLE: Because they want to think that they're the center and that their world matters. No, ignore that, my friend. You as a man lead. And whether it's the woman he's got now, and it sounds to me like there's some shakiness going on, I could be wrong. I'm not saying it either way. Somebody will come and find you and follow you and you'll say, "I like this girl."

STEFANIA: Well, you have to be worthy of following. Being followed I should say.

BEN SETTLE: And they'll hang around and he'll test the hell out of her as I tested you. See, I just flipped the script. Most girls naturally test guys. They're always looking for a reason to get rid of a dude.

STEFANIA: Right like in *Top Gun*.

BEN SETTLE: Absolutely. Yeah.

STEFANIA: In that scene she was being tested by Maverick.

BEN SETTLE: Absolutely. But I think a guy has to do that because as a guy Stefania, everything I have to offer is more special and more valuable than the physical that you offer on the front end. I'm talking about, let me be very clear. I'm talking about the front end.

STEFANIA: I know what you mean.

BEN SETTLE: Not for you, for the shrieking Karen listening to this right now. Okay? The wine aunt that's drowning herself in wine and chocolate because she bought into lies that are rapidly leaving otherwise perfectly fine women at 52 years old with nothing but a job and a Match.com account instead of a husband and children that love her.

STEFANIA: Well, my beauty is very…

BEN SETTLE: Your beauty is what?

STEFANIA: Is fleeting.

BEN SETTLE: Exactly. It's fleeting, but it gets you in on the front end.

STEFANIA: In 30 years I don't know how you'll feel about me.

BEN SETTLE: I'll tell you why, because guys, and I've seen study after study on this. When a guy is with a woman, as your looks fade, we don't notice it that much. We just don't. Look at Hugh Jackman.

STEFANIA: He loves her.

BEN SETTLE: He loves that woman. She's 10 years older, out of shape, he's jacked and voted sexiest man alive. But he loves her.

STEFANIA: If you read any of the interviews, she has his back. She will tear down reporters when they try to talk shit...

BEN SETTLE: And you know who else does that? And I never thought I'd say this, is Zuckerberg's wife.

STEFANIA: Yeah, she does.

BEN SETTLE: She actually has that guy's back.

STEFANIA: She's his human shield.

BEN SETTLE: And you're my human shield.

STEFANIA: Yes I am.

BEN SETTLE: When I took you to seminars, I dragged you to seminars against your will.

STEFANIA: Oh yeah. Because I hated going down to Napa. I hated going down to Delray Beach. Oh, I was so mad. Oh man, I have to be down in Florida. Oh, fuck this.

BEN SETTLE: And I'm telling you, you were my human shield.

STEFANIA: I was.

BEN SETTLE: And see that's the thing, it was beyond just pretty and all that. Pretty women are a dime a dozen. You need it to get in on the front end, it's still important. Even vital. But at the end of the day pretty women are a commodity. Millions of 'em out there. And guys who have reached a certain level of success and confidence are not. You're the woman, you tell me. If they were so abundant, you'd be swimming in all these options. And you are swimming in options?

STEFANIA: Women are swimming in options.

BEN SETTLE: But they're not the options you want.

STEFANIA: No. Especially here, some of them might not have all their teeth. They might be homeless. I don't know.

BEN SETTLE: Every time I leave, if I so much as get my hair cut, you sweat a little bit. Why? You sweat? You do not want another woman taking me. It bothers you. Hold on, before you look at me as if I'm crazy. We were watching *Deep Space 9* yesterday. And Miles O'Brien's wife was trying to get him to hang out with Kira, because they transferred her baby to her. They want...

STEFANIA: She's a surrogate basically. Yeah.

BEN SETTLE: Yeah. And they started kind of falling for each other. And you said what? Something about proximity.

STEFANIA: Yeah. It happens. Proximity. Like you say, familiarity breeds contempt. It also breeds this kind of shit. And I've seen it so many times in so many different ways in the store my mom owns in Manhattan, hearing stories.

BEN SETTLE: You got to say what the store is, so there's context. Very important.

STEFANIA: My mom owns a luxury resale boutique in Manhattan. And she has for the last 20 some odd years, since 2001. And I basically grew up in the store. That's where I cut my teeth in business, all that. So being there, I've heard a lot of stories because women talk. Whenever they're among other women, they'll just talk about things. I know way more about people than I should. And so, when it comes to relationships, when it comes to infidelity, I've seen all sides, right? I've seen guys come in with their wives and their girlfriends later to the same store. My mom just doesn't say anything. Or I've seen women who they were the starter wives. And the trophy wives come in, also the other women come into the store and they always talk about whatever 's going on. And when it comes to proximity, and I had this experience and don't harrumph me. Even when—

BEN SETTLE: I don't harrumph. These are lesser men, you think I care?

STEFANIA: But There's a reason I bring this up. I was dating a neurologist who worked at one of the, I don't know, you call it brother hospital, sister hospital to where one of my mom 's friends was a nurse at and she told me, she says, "Oh, so you're dating this guy," whatever. "You have to bring him lunch. You have to make an appearance at the hospital because nurses, because of the proximity they will, if they did not already have their eye on him, they're going to want to." Because, I'm not saying it because all these nurses are these harlots or something. I'm not saying that, but it's just—

BEN SETTLE: It's...

STEFANIA: ... it's proximity because they're working 20 hour shifts together. They're doing all sorts of hair raising harrowing shit. And they're just...

BEN SETTLE: The adrenaline, the hormones, all that mixing together.

STEFANIA: Oh, yeah. It's all of it.

BEN SETTLE: The excitement.

STEFANIA: Yeah. There's excitement. There's grief. There're all sorts of really...

BEN SETTLE: They share emotions.

STEFANIA: Yeah.

BEN SETTLE: If another woman shares an emotion with me, how do you react?

STEFANIA: I would...

BEN SETTLE: You would go what?

STEFANIA: Feral.

BEN SETTLE: Unless it's my mother, no woman's allowed to share an emotion with me. Why? Because you've seen this happen.

STEFANIA: Yeah, yeah. So, that's what I'm saying. The advice I was given by that nurse was that, if I want to keep this guy, bring him lunch, make your face known at the hospital, so that way the nurses know to back off. And she told me straight up as somebody who's been a nurse for like 4,000 years, She's like, that's how it works.

BEN SETTLE: You remember when I said that this would do women no good? Actually, you just did.

STEFANIA: Maybe.

BEN SETTLE: You just gave great advice for women.

STEFANIA: And I've seen the same thing when I was a paralegal. When I was in the legal field with attorneys, there's proximity. Right? Because you're going through… The whole work husband, work wife thing. That's an example of proximity.

BEN SETTLE: This kind of relates to something else I heard. And it's important. It's important people understand that I heard you say this. Because I get accused of being a sexist and misogynist for it, and I at least want some accuracy here. One thing you have said, and you totally pulled this out of your ass one day. We were walking to downtown in Bandon, and you said, "If you want to please the man ask the mistress, not the wife."

STEFANIA: Right.

BEN SETTLE: Explain. Because I thought that was very profound in a lot of ways.

STEFANIA: And I didn't mean it to be. It's just when a husband is cheating on his wife, it's because it's out of escapism. There's something in the home that he's seeking, something else. Right? Could be his wife...

BEN SETTLE: It's very expensive just to leave a wife.

STEFANIA: Right. And I say, okay. So one of...

BEN SETTLE: Especially if there's kids involved.

STEFANIA: Right. One of my friends from law school, and I told you about her, I won't name her. She—

BEN SETTLE: The one with the grandma legs?

STEFANIA: Yeah, I know.

BEN SETTLE: That's what your mom said. I didn't.

STEFANIA: My mom said she had grandma legs.

BEN SETTLE: All right. Well, go ahead.

STEFANIA: So she was stepping around with a married man. And he was a very, very well-known partner in the industry that we were in. So it was a really big deal that she was with this guy. She wasn't a paralegal or anything, but she was in a similar industry with him. So again, proximity, they were in the same circles and they saw each other enough and blah, blah, blah. And then shit happened. And she would tell me about it because people like to tell me things. This is in law school. But I've also seen this also in the store too because the other women would come in and tell me or tell my mom what stuff. So they would always talk about what it is. Whenever they talk about their relationship, and this is like, you can almost bet on it. They'll immediately go into one, what they see in the guy, and then what the wife is not giving to them. And because it's a justification like, "Well, I'm with him, because his wife really, she ignores his needs or She's never really there, or there's no love in the relationship."

BEN SETTLE: In other words—

STEFANIA: They always try to justify it.

BEN SETTLE: ...the guy has a world and the wife has either taken it for granted, and does not appreciate it. Or the guy, obviously the guy could just be a player.

STEFANIA: Right. And like goomas. Right?

BEN SETTLE: And she took it for granted.

STEFANIA: Yeah.

BEN SETTLE: And he's like, "well, I can do better than this, but he can't just leave her."

STEFANIA: Right. And...

BEN SETTLE: And this is what people don't get. This stuff happens and all they want to do is blame the guy, but they never look at what did she do? He's done everything he's supposed to do. What has she done? She let herself go. She got fat. She stopped caring what he thinks. She becomes an insufferable cunt, which is the worst thing she could do. The reason you're with me, Stefania, the main reason is because you have always had my back.

STEFANIA: Yeah.

BEN SETTLE: These exes, you know none of them have had my back. Not really. They did temporarily when it suited them. But eventually their solipsism kicks in and I'm like, "This ain't going to work. If they act like this now with the dumb mood swings, how bad will it get later when I can't easily escape? I can't give this person my ultimate commitment." This is advice for the guy here. I'm not living in another woman's world catering to her lunacy, her every lunatic mood change and all that. I'm solidly based here. I got my things going. I can't be torn and distracted like that. I got to be able to focus on what I'm going after.

STEFANIA: Right.

BEN SETTLE: Like the story Ken McCarthy told you of how he got into Dan Kennedy's world.

STEFANIA: Oh yeah.

BEN SETTLE: In one word, he said he was useful to Dan Kennedy. That's how he became Dan's internet marketing guy, the only one Dan trusted. Now obviously it's a different time.

STEFANIA: Well, right. But...

BEN SETTLE: But that's what you are.

STEFANIA: It's true. He really appreciated being around Dan Kennedy.

BEN SETTLE: He said, he was in his world.

STEFANIA: He was in his world.

BEN SETTLE: He liked it there.

STEFANIA: And he liked him and he was like, how can I be helpful? Genuinely helpful.

BEN SETTLE: Genuinely. It was not...

STEFANIA: Not like, "oh, well, I think you need this."

BEN SETTLE: And that's the difference. That's the difference, Stefania. I can tell you, other women I've dated, even ones who for more than one or two years, whatever, they were not genuinely useful past a certain point. They started going into wanting me to go to their world, fighting me on it, and no longer being a useful helper but an antagonistic distraction and a problem. And so now it's a drag on me. You have not been that way. You came into my world and you, A, didn't want to leave. And B, you were like, how can I make this world even better?

STEFANIA: Yeah.

BEN SETTLE: "What can I do, Ben, to make this world better?" And that is what I appreciate. And not a day goes by where I don't thank you for making me good meals, for taking care of Willis, right? Taking care of Zoe especially in her dotage right now, taking care of the house. Not a day goes by where I don't thank you for that.

STEFANIA: No.

BEN SETTLE: No, because it's genuine. And you do it from a place of love, whatever. And so to answer this guy's question, it's not about all these things. "How do I get her to do this and that?" You be a leader and just be the guy. Don't be needy. Understand you're the prize. And I say this and guys are like, "I don't feel like the prize." Well, they got to figure that out. Technique will only get you so far, you got to get your head on straight.

STEFANIA: Right. Well, that comes to knowing what it is that their game is. Now, if you become... I know it sounds so simple.

BEN SETTLE: Right. It does sound simple and it's not simple.

STEFANIA: But it's not simple.

BEN SETTLE: But it does sound simple.

STEFANIA: Yeah. Instead of going, looking outwardly, like "what can I do for people to like me?" Or "what can I do for people to think I'm XYZ," whatever it is, right? Like the internet marketers and what car should I drive...

BEN SETTLE: What mansion in the third world country should I be renting to try to look like I have money when really I'm broke right now?

STEFANIA: Right.

BEN SETTLE: These idiot third world gringos.

STEFANIA: Oh my goodness.

BEN SETTLE: All these Bali guys. The Philippines, wherever the hell these people are.

STEFANIA: So...

BEN SETTLE: Living on $2 a day and acting like they're Kings when they couldn't even afford a decent place in a medium sized city in a first world country, while pretending to be successful.

STEFANIA: I know, right? For me when they're one political upheaval away from having to flee.

BEN SETTLE: Anyway, go ahead. What were you going to say?

STEFANIA: So, there was even a bunch of them that they defaulted in student loans. And so they actually can't come back to the United States. So, there's that. So for you, you already were set in your ways, right? But you had to know what your ways were first in order to be set.

BEN SETTLE: I told you, if I had met you even 10 years ago, it would not have worked.

STEFANIA: Right.

BEN SETTLE: And it is what it is. But I'm telling you, guy has to focus on himself first, get your body in shape. Right?

STEFANIA: Mm-hmm.

BEN SETTLE: Get yourself physically, mentally, and spiritually, get right with God. All right. Don't go to Bali and worship Baphomet at the volcanoes and all that. Don't do that. Find Jesus and reject all the pagan idolatry bull shit the culture pushes. And do it and just lead. And that's my whole point. Lead your life. Talk to women that you find interesting. Follow your passions and interests, and really just do those three things. That builds a world some women will not be interested in, but others will. And you can then pick one out of those that do like it. And keep improving yourself and put that first and understand that, and this is going to get me in trouble, Stefania, but it's absolute truth. You've got to love her a little less than she loves you. Stefania, if I was fawning all over you more than you fawn over me—

STEFANIA: Oh my God, no.

BEN SETTLE: ...it would drive you nuts.

STEFANIA: I've been in relationships where guys...

BEN SETTLE: You don't like that.

STEFANIA: No, I don't.

BEN SETTLE: You like that I'm a little hard to get, but you don't really know. You're a little insecure. I leave for Kung Fu for the day and you're wondering if I'm stopping at someone's house for some ass somewhere.

STEFANIA: Oh, no. That's not what I think, but I do want you to come home because I miss you. And that's the thing, I miss you when you leave for the day.

BEN SETTLE: I have to make something clear. When I say you got to love them a little less than they love you, I'm not saying you got to be cruel. I'm saying you have to have something to reach for. She can't just be your little world and you're orbiting around her. It's her job to orbit around you. Now I can already hear the harrowing screams of the single wine moms and wine aunts listening to this. And that's good. This is the first step toward them finding love in their lives.

STEFANIA: Here's something that also, I don't know if he's doing it. From what you read, it didn't sound like that's what he's doing. But I do know there's again, going to that, doing things that you think people want. Like, if you asked me before I met you, what I wanted in a guy, it might not have been you.

BEN SETTLE: Oh, your checklist would've been the opposite of me.

STEFANIA: It was the opposite of you. It totally was the opposite of you.

BEN SETTLE: And all your friends were like, "He just sits in his house cleaning guns all day." First of all, I wish that was true.

STEFANIA: No, no.

BEN SETTLE: I wish I had a bunker like that. I don't.

STEFANIA: No. One person who was at the time, an Email Players subscriber, she told me that all you did was collect cash and guns. And you were like a doomsday prepper or something.

BEN SETTLE: And I'm like, I aspire to be that. That actually inspired me.

STEFANIA: And you're like...

BEN SETTLE: I was like, you know what? I could use some more guns.

STEFANIA: That's all you did. It was just like hoard guns and cash.

BEN SETTLE: Thank you, Lisa.

STEFANIA: Like Smaug or something or something weird.

BEN SETTLE: Yeah. And I like Smaug.

STEFANIA: And I was like, really?

BEN SETTLE: I know. And I am in the Lonely Mountain.

STEFANIA: Right.

BEN SETTLE: Absolutely. It is lonely here. And I like it that way.

STEFANIA: But if you asked me like, "Stefania, what would you..." Not even Stefania, I was Stefanie then, right?

BEN SETTLE: Yeah. I knighted you "Stefania."

STEFANIA: Right.

BEN SETTLE: For the record.

STEFANIA: But if you asked me, I would've said I wanted to be with an extrovert who would want to do all the things I wanted to do. Who was adventurous, who loved traveling.

BEN SETTLE: And who love voting Democrat.

STEFANIA: Right. Because those are all the things that I thought I wanted and those were the things I had before. And then I meet you, who hates all of those things. And then I'm like, huh. You can't directly ask a woman what she wants is what I'm saying. She will align with you if that's something that she...

BEN SETTLE: And this is a good way to round it out, because I want to end with one little story. The first time I ever spoke to you was on Skype.

STEFANIA: Mm-hmm. A couple weeks before you came here for that event.

BEN SETTLE: And you were complaining to me about law school. This is very important, because I was detached from it. I didn't make your problems my problems. You told me some guys did that.

STEFANIA: Yeah. I couldn't tell them anything.

BEN SETTLE: They would start crying because something happened to you and they would take it harder than you did.

STEFANIA: Right. And when something terrible happened to me, I had to console them because they were so distraught that this happened to me and I'm like, "the hell is wrong with you?"

BEN SETTLE: And that's an example of the guy loving you more than you love him.

STEFANIA: Yeah. That was really upsetting.

BEN SETTLE: Now, when I talked to you, you were talking about law school because it sucked. And I said, "Then why are you going?" And a week later you quit law school. I didn't know how to feel about that at the time. I was like, "wait minute. Well, hold on."

STEFANIA: I know. Your stepmom, Mama Coe was like, "Why did you do that to her?" And I was like, "he didn't do anything to me. He just confirmed the thing that I was feeling." I remember, I was telling you the equivalent of like writing pages upon pages upon pages of explaining the problem, explaining all the things I was feeling.

BEN SETTLE: And I simply asked, "So why don't you just leave?"

STEFANIA: And then you summarize it into one sentence.

BEN SETTLE: You were doing good money with the copywriting and branding stuff. And that's my point. I just kind of gave you something to go on. I led you into my world.

STEFANIA: Well, you were truly an objective person, because you didn't give a shit what I did.

BEN SETTLE: No. It didn't bother me. I don't care.

STEFANIA: Yeah.

BEN SETTLE: But that's the point. You can't go to a woman and sit there and suffocate her. You got to be candid. And you know what? It may be your job to lead her from going astray. And I'm just going to leave it at that. Unless you have something else you want to add, Stefania. You know what? I'm going to do something for you I've never done before. I'm going to let you have the last word.

STEFANIA: Oh my goodness.

BEN SETTLE: You go right ahead, Stefania. You go right ahead.

STEFANIA: Well, if you're going to say, leading her from going astray, if She's going to go astray, She's going to go astray. All you can do is just say like, "Well, listen, this is what I have going." That's what you did to me.

BEN SETTLE: Yes.

STEFANIA: You were like, "this is my life, here's where I'm going, you can join me or not."

BEN SETTLE: Yes. "I may let you come with, but you come here, we'll test it out. You tell me what you think. I don't think you'll like it." Which none of that was a lie by the way. I really didn't think you'd like where I was living, and all that.

STEFANIA: Right. You weren't even doing a negative strip line. You were just like...

BEN SETTLE: I mean it was, but not as a tactic.

STEFANIA: Right. It wasn't like a persuasion thing. You were like, "No, really. I don't think you'd like it out here."

BEN SETTLE: Because I had enough respect for you to be honest with you.

STEFANIA: Right.

BEN SETTLE: And everybody wants honesty until you tell them the truth.

STEFANIA: That's true. But you being honest intrigued me and I could 've made a decision like, "oh, Ben is not really my speed" but you showed me enough of your life. And that showed me you were not trying to do it to impress me. You just, you said, "This is my world. You take it or leave it." And I was intrigued enough because it was so different from what I was used to, that you showed me options for different thinking.

BEN SETTLE: Which was a Patrice O'Neal thing. I give him full credit for that. But it's very true. I mean, that's really what you got to do.

STEFANIA: Yeah. And I could have decided for myself like, "No, I'm going to remain in new York," or not. And then I realized you showed me a different way that I could be doing things, that I could be living. And I glommed onto it and I appreciated it because I didn't know that's what I was looking for. So, I know in his question, he was saying like, "How do I get a girl to invest?" You can't ask outright. Right? Because like I said, if you'd asked me...

BEN SETTLE: You don't get her to do anything, you invite her in. You will do what you're going to do with or without her either way.

STEFANIA: And if she likes it, she likes it.

BEN SETTLE: She likes it, she'll say, and you've almost got to try to get rid of her. That's what I did. I tried getting rid of you, giving you reasons to say no.

STEFANIA: Right. And you can't do the whole...

BEN SETTLE: And I've done that. By the way, I've done that with other girls too, that I've dated. I would think of reasons to get rid of them. And I think this is an important thing. You have to try to break things, right? It's the Scientific Method. You're not trying to prove something, you're trying to disprove it. And I think that's very applicable to this. I was trying to find reasons to get rid of you. You stubbornly would not give me any reason. And when you find that woman, you're good to go. Because most women are not going to do that for every guy.

STEFANIA: Right.

BEN SETTLE: They're not going to do that for just any guy, and nor should they.

STEFANIA: No. And here's a good point, because even I told you, I dated someone before who was from the Pacific Northwest.

BEN SETTLE: Yes, you did. They know you around here far and wide, Stefania.

STEFANIA: Oh, stop it. He was from Washington. He lived in New York though. And he was always talking about how he wanted me to move to Tacoma with him. And I was always intrigued by the Pacific Northwest. And I always...

BEN SETTLE: But you were not intrigued by him.

STEFANIA: No. And even, I always loved the idea of the area and I'd never been here before. So even when you being here, I was like, oh, okay. I want to come. Because I always wanted to come out here, but I didn't want to go with him. And so it's, how do I say this? Like I said before, you can't ask somebody outright, but at the same time it could be that even if she is in a different place, like I in a very different place than I am now. And it's hard for me to even imagine how I was before I met you.

BEN SETTLE: And now you're in even a more remote place than Bandon.

STEFANIA: Right.

BEN SETTLE: And you were the one that helped find this place for me. You have been useful. And this is very important for people to hear.

STEFANIA: Because most guys I've...

BEN SETTLE: I don't have time to chase your moods and emotions around.

STEFANIA: No. And also, some guys are like, "what can I do to impress her?"

BEN SETTLE: Have I ever tried to impress you?

STEFANIA: No. And even...

BEN SETTLE: So, I'm saying, a guy has to make a world that the girl wants to enter. And most women will not want to enter. Guys got to understand that. And once you stop caring what any one girl thinks it just becomes way easier and more fun. In fact, you're going to have too many options probably. And I'll end it with that because I know you don't want to hear that part.

STEFANIA: I thought I was supposed to have the last word.

BEN SETTLE: Well, once again, I have usurped and so be it.

BizWorld Typology

Training from the prestigious Profit Pirates coaching program.
www.EmailPlayers.com/pirates

BEN SETTLE: I don't know how many of you guys have Social Lair, the book, you don't need it for what we're going to talk about. But if you do have it, a lot of this will make sense. Apparently, Stefania, I wasn't as clear in this book as I should have been about one thing. Yesterday. Today is what Wednesday? Yeah it was yesterday.

STEFANIA: Yeah.

BEN SETTLE: Okay, so I get my days mixed up. Andre was on here and he was asking me a question that I thought I was clear about on the book but I may not have been. And so, if you do have the book it's a good time to get clarification on stuff that I may have just dropped the ball with. I wrote that book really fast. I wrote it in 19 days—literally. So, I'm sure I missed a few things.

STEFANIA: Well, one thing about the book is, what was it that Captain Call in Lonesome Dove says? It's better to have it and not need it than to need it and not have it. Is that what it was?

BEN SETTLE: Yeah. Yeah. Just like having a Latina. Better to have a Latina and not need one than to need a Latina and not have one.

STEFANIA: <laughter>

BEN SETTLE: Look, all of you guys as Profit Pirates are going to have a Lair as part of your Profit Pirates subscription, whether you want to use it or not is up to you obviously. But I dare say everything that we talk about you could use even on inferior platforms of course like Facebook. So, that's where I cut my teeth and so be it.

STEFANIA: Is that what the confusion came from?

BEN SETTLE: No, the confusion was he wanted to know if he has more of a laid back personality and he doesn't want to fight people, if he doesn't want brawl and all that, he doesn't want berserkers going around sharpening their swords and trying to kill each other. What if you're just a regular human being and you still want to create conflict, but you don't want to do it the way I do it? All you have got to do is have an opinion. That's all you have got to do is have an opinion. Having an opinion automatically creates conflict.

STEFANIA: So, actually that's a good point where we could start, because where I originally wanted to talk about was you being an introvert and because most people think like, oh to have social media I need to be an extrovert, I need to be all over the place and Gary Vee creating like 2,000 pieces of content a day. So, let's start with that part about if you want to just be a normal guy, a normal person and just not have people banging on their shields and collecting heads, because it was that bad, but you say, "oh it wasn't that bad," but it was that bad. And so what would your advice be to somebody who wants to create conflict but not blood struggling conflict?

BEN SETTLE: I'll just reiterate what I told Andre that I said just have an opinion. But it can't be an opinion that everybody agrees with. You got to have disagreement, otherwise there's no conflict. But here's something I did and I didn't do it on purpose, but it was the effect—and that is to surround yourself in your social media, wherever it is, with extroverts and people who do want to go out and fight and berserk on your behalf. That was the key. For example, Stefania, I had you. You were one of several and you were not shy about giving your opinion. Nicole was never shy about giving her opinion. And Nicole had gone into some really crazy if I remember correctly. She was defending cheating, not so much defending it, but giving a point of view about why it happens.

And I said now that was perfect. She wasn't defending it, but she made a case for it. I wanted stuff that nobody could ignore it and it would be almost a little uncomfortable publicly disagreeing with it or publicly agreeing with something. But see it doesn't have to be a fight or a drag out. You don't have to do any of it. You can just instigate, you set the fire and let the other people throw the fuel on because they want to, they're looking, most people are out there looking for something that they can engage with. That's why they're on there. Now you have your lurkers and all that too. I'd probably be more of a lurker in any other situation if it wasn't my own thing and that's fine. Sometimes they can be useful too, I guess.

And I'll say something else here, Stefania. And this is something I noticed in elBenbo's Lair. And I notice this just on Facebook in general and I've noticed this in other social networking type atmospheres that an awful lot of introverts actually become extroverts on the internet. It's almost like an outlet for them. And so just because someone's introverted doesn't mean they're not going to be chatty and actually be the most engaged people. Because they might just be.

STEFANIA: Can you talk a little bit more about that? Because I'm not an introvert, so I can't pretend to be one or I understand how you operate but it doesn't mean I can explain how you can go between the two. Because I usually see you with your hood up, your sunglasses on, your hat on looking like the Unabomber not wanting to talk to anyone. And there's other introverts I've seen in the lair that we're in there like 24/7. It made me wonder if they work, did they eat, did they shower, did they sleep.

BEN SETTLE: I think it was their safe social life. There was a social life without having to go anywhere, which ultimately comes down to World-Building. See, and I wanted to talk about, I'm going to force World-Building into this even if it's not natural, because I'm giving a presentation to Brian Kurtz's mastermind tomorrow and I want it fresh in my mind. But if any of you have read the Narnia books or watched the Narnia movies, it doesn't matter either one. Or if you're at least familiar with them enough that you know what they are. Do you notice how when they went to Narnia, when the kids went to Narnia, which was sometimes a place of deadly danger, it was not always this, in fact that was the whole point. There was a very real possibly they could die a horrible death. Yet they never wanted to leave Narnia.

Aslan created a world that people didn't want to leave. And when they left they got very... almost depressed. In fact, Susan from the first two movies if you just saw the movies, she can't come back after Prince Caspian. And in the books, the last book, you find out she ends up becoming bitter about it to the point where she pretends she never went there. She makes fun of her siblings forever talking about it and She's not a friend of the place. She almost becomes a troll of Narnia in some ways. And that's how you know you're doing it right. Because when you kick people out and you don't let them back in, they can get very mad. They have to deserve it. I don't think you should necessarily just do it, but the whole point is to create a world that people don't want to leave. And so, if you do that, you're already 99% ahead of everybody and especially the introvert, because you've now given them a place to go.

They don't have to go to the local tavern now. They don't have to go anywhere. They don't have to force themselves to go do stuff. I'm not even saying this is a healthy thing by the way. I'm not claiming that because I wonder about this actually. But that's the key. So, what can you do? And this is going to be different for everybody and this is why there's no checklist. There is no checklist to World-Building and this is especially on the internet because it comes from within. And I've been doing a lot of thinking about this and I was thinking about the best world builder ever from the most part that I've seen in business would be Walt Disney. And you know a Disney product, property, whatever, when you see one, there's no question. Even the live action movies, especially back in the sixties, you knew it was a Disney movie, just had a certain flavor to it. And he literally created the Disneyland, which is literally a world you go to, to spend a lot of money, happily spend money, nobody resents being sold inside that world, even though it's designed to extract as much money from you as possible… and yet you don't want to leave.

And I think about stuff like that. But that whole Disneyland in his whole Disney studio, the whole world he created, nobody taught him how to do it. It went back to his childhood. He just really wanted to create the environment that he grew up in, this small town that he really loved that it's like he was chasing it his whole life and the company he built and the community of workers he hired, Disneyland and all that was his way of recreating it. And I think it comes from somewhere within. Apple originally was a very well created world, too. I think they peaked when Steve Jobs died and I think it's going down fast now. But it had a very specific culture. He used to even make fun of Bill Gates saying Microsoft has no culture, no soul.

With Apple Steve Jobs created a world his fans don't want to leave, to the point where about 10 years ago they took a bunch of Apple buyers and they put their brains under these magnetic whatever things where they could read their brainwaves and saw their brains react to an Apple gadget like they would react to whatever deity they worship. It's literally a religion for them. That's World-Building right there. And Nobody can teach it as a structured thing. I mean, there's stuff you can do. People have my elBenbo Press and Social Lair and Brand Barbarian and Markauteur books where I'm giving you enough to go on to get started. But really there's got to be a unique something there from the start. And with Jobs, it just started with a frustration. He was a craftsman.

His dad instilled in him this craftsmanship thing and he could not stand seeing IBM and just all the crap out there and he just knew he could do better. And it started with that. With Disney it started with the longing for where he grew up. For me it was like a whole difference. I don't even know where the hell mine came from quite frankly it just was there. Probably just from being frustrated with what I see around me in real life and on the internet and all that. I wanted to create a place I wanted to be. As a business, people should create a world where they want to be, that their customers will love being just like Apple and Disney customers love going to those worlds. Just like people who watch Mister Rogers and the world of make believe he wanted to be in—the world he created. And same with what Jim Henson and others have done. And so I don't know, this is more of a beacon than anything else. But if you think about that with wherever you're going to be on social media, create a place that's uniquely you. It shouldn't be based on anything anyone else has done.

I just give frameworks when I discuss this. I mean, you could do the same stuff I did, but you got to still own it as your own expression. Like in kung fu Sifu teaches that. He's like, we all learn the exact same principles, we all learn the exact same forms and system. But we all express it uniquely. I'm going to express kung fu a little bit, maybe a lot differently, than he would. My physical attributes are different. Someone who has one leg is going to express it differently. He's going to have to, by just definition of what is. Someone who's heavier set is going to express it differently. Someone who's more hyper is going to express it differently than someone who's laid back. Someone who's short will express it differently than someone who's tall. Someone who's ripped will express it differently than someone who is skinny. Someone who's a faster thinker will express it differently than someone who is a slower thinker. Someone with a higher IQ will express it different than someone with a lower IQ. Someone who likes the footwork will express it different from someone who prefers striking. And that's my whole point. It comes from you, and how you express it, and you start with that and you start with one thing.

If you don't know where to start, I talked about Narnia and building a world you didn't want to leave. And even as a reader, as a kid, I didn't want to leave those books and I know a lot of other people were the same way. C.S. Lewis didn't have that world figured out. He literally just had an image in his head of a faun in the forest with a bunch of presents. How the book starts basically. And he built from there. He didn't have anything figured out beyond that to start. I know Tolkien didn't have jack figured out either. People think he had this whole thing figured out. It took him 20 freaking years to figure it out. You should see some of the ideas he came up with first. All he wanted to do was write about hobbits eating. That was Lord of the Rings. And I'm not even exaggerating. The Hobbit, he said when they got out of the Misty Mountains he wasn't even sure where they were going to go next. He just let it unfold.

And I think that's part of the fun actually. I'm doing it in Learnistic right now, it's a little slower going as I'm not as engaged with it as I'd like to be. But We've been doing it slowly even with Learnistic. It's just something you feel your way through. And I know none of this is a direct answer. It may even create more questions for people. But this is the start of it. It's just to start to get people thinking differently. Most people go on social media and they're like, "okay I got to socialize, I got to give value or I got to teach."

None of that is necessarily right or wrong. But think of it as a world you create within your own pocket dimension, your own alternate reality. You have unlimited powers to a certain degree to create it how you want. You're a kid playing with toys. Playing with toys is going to create little worlds. But it starts with that first toy, then that toy interacting with another toy. Then it starts a chain reaction with other toys until you have a whole world going on of toys. That's how you look at it. And it just starts with one thing, one wrong you want to right or just one thing you're trying to recapture, one thing that you wish was out there that's not that you wish was there in social media or anywhere else and start with that.

STEFANIA: So, all right so Danielle says, "I mentioned this yesterday and while I don't like it as they think it's rather cowardly, a lot of people create conflict by starting their own post/email off with, "I don't mean to create conflict, but …" and then they say something that's so mainstream it's like please. Yeah, I think it actually works because people, boring people flock to boring people.

BEN SETTLE: Danielle, do you actually see that work on social media where they get a lot of engagement doing that? I seriously don't know because I haven't been on any social media in a while, but I would be the first one to troll a post like that.

DANIELLE: That's funny that you say that, because I've been actually thinking I'm going to create conflict by actually commenting on those posts when I see internet marketers do that, that are so boring. And it's like all you do is regurgitate the same thing that a hundred of you are saying. So, actually you just came up with another perfect way to create conflict. But that is genuine. Because I find that very annoying as a consumer of various products and things. I'm tired of people pitching me stuff that is presented as something but it's really something else. So, I think that's fair.

BEN SETTLE: And that could potentially be what you build a world around quite frankly, if that's something that bothers you. That could be something you build around. That could be your Mr. Tumnus trotting around the forest like C.S. Lewis had the image in his head that you build upon. I just throw that out there because it is a real thing and it applies to every market. It doesn't have to be internet marketing. I bet you Grace has the same thing in the dog market. People just being milquetoast and plain vanilla but pretending they have something controversial to say.

STEFANIA: Yeah, and Grace actually, she commented, "isn't that a decent attempt of negative strip line?" I don't think so. But you are the expert.

BEN SETTLE: No, not the way I'm saying it at least. Negative strip line is where it's like they're going to be skeptical of something you're about to say and you subvert it, and you become even more negative than they are. "What I'm about to tell you is probably the dumbest thing you could ever listen to. Quite frankly, what I'm about to say is so stupid that it will probably lower your IQ. However, there is a chance that it may be the best idea you ever get about stopping your dog's farting…" So, here it is. You just triple down on whatever it is that they're already skeptical about, and you not only agree with that negativity but amplify that negativity. So I'm not sure if that applies to World-Building, but it can certainly be done within your World-Building adventures.

STEFANIA: What they're saying is not really controversial anyway so they're not being skeptical about it, there's not even anything to strip.

BEN SETTLE: They'd be better off saying, "look, I'm going to be honest with you guys. What I'm about to say is what everybody says. It is going to be so boring and routine that it would put you to sleep except for…" and then you throw in some little zinger that just shocks the hell out of them. I don't know what that would be, because this is all hypothetical, but you're just meeting them at their skepticism and you're saying they're absolutely right to be skeptical, and that you are even more skeptical than they are. But if they hear you out, it will be worth it for them. One of the reasons you may or may not notice that I do this a lot is I always tell people I'm very biased about what I'm about to say. Why? Because it's obvious I'm selling something. Of course, I'm biased. So, you might as well just admit it and if possible, double down on it when it makes sense.

STEFANIA: That makes sense. Okay, so there's two things that you said I would like to pick up on. One of them is that when you're talking about building your Narnia, and this is something that you did in Enoch Wars, and I'm not saying that to plug Enoch Wars, but —

BEN SETTLE: Hold on, hold on, hold on, hold on. I'm taking time out of my precious day to be here. I am plugging Enoch Wars. The books are being turned into audio books. All right, plug over. But you can get into the world I created with Enoch Wars inside the mobile app I made for it at www.EnochWars.com.

STEFANIA: We've talked about the influences that you've had in writing these books and also some things where I'm like, we're watching something. I'm like, oh I could feel a little bit, this is a little Enoch Wars this and you're like, "I didn't even think about that." Is that when you wrote Enoch Wars, you basically, you had those, that story outline, you knew what you wanted to do, but you wrote about shit that you liked. You wrote it in the style that you liked. You wrote about storylines you liked, you included villains that you liked. And it wasn't like, "oh because I want to present this bigger picture because I wanted to have this outcome." You just wrote what you liked and what you enjoyed and what you yourself wanted to read.

BEN SETTLE: And there's another aspect to that though. And this is, I don't like giving Stephen King a lot of credit, because I actually think he's an intellectual lightweight. I enjoy some of his books, don't get me wrong, but the person himself… I read his Twitter and wonder, "how can this guy be as dumb as a box of rocks?" I haven't read anything since his last *Dark Tower* book, which was the biggest disappointment ever. Because you talk about building a world and then actually building this really cool thing and then making it like, "oh that was a waste of time…"

He didn't really say this but he's the one I heard it from, so I'm going to give him credit for it. But I'm sure he was quoting someone else when he said writers write the books they wish someone else had written but nobody wrote it so we know we just have to write it. And I'd say that's the same with World-Building. That's exactly it. He did an NPR interview once and he summed up the idea of World-Building very, very succinctly. And I think this applies to what I was saying before, building a world they don't want to leave. That's what he says. When he sits down to write, he goes 20 hours a day I live in the regular ordinary world like everybody else. But during the four hours a day he writes, he enters a world that's completely different and wonderful and fascinating.

It's just completely his own playground. And I remember thinking that's exactly how to think about World-Building to apply it to your business. I've got this saying now, "don't build businesses, build worlds", because a business can be boarded up. A business can be de platformed. A business has competition. A business can be taken down by the attorney general. A business can be quite frankly destroyed. A business can be blown up in some cases. A business can be blown up by rioters in Portland. A world really can't. If you build your own world, it can't really, even after your death, it's not necessarily going to die if you do it right. And I like to think in these types of bigger terms because it should give you comfort that if you build the world right that people want to come to, where they find you, and they don't want to leave, selling really isn't that big of a deal anymore.

It's not only more fun for you and for them, but the selling is almost secondary. It's automatic. You don't really have to worry about it all that much as long as you're not really screwing up. I think of our Wine Villains event Troy and I did. If that wasn't the best example of how selling happens when you build a world I don't know what is. I barely even pitched the damn thing and we sold out, standing room only, having people fly in some cases from all around the world to show up. And all I did was maybe put up a few posts about it. I didn't hard sell it. We didn't even know what we were going to teach, because they weren't there for that. They were there because they'd been in this world I built, they wanted to hang out with me.

But even more, I think they wanted to hang out with each other, because they're citizens in this society, in this world. And they built real friendships, and you can't engineer that with direct response marketing. You really can't. When I talk to direct marketers about this tomorrow, I think some of them will be very disappointed by this, because what direct marketers want is everything to be quantified and tracked and all that. And in some ways I share their frustration. But you can't track it. It's just something that comes from within and you start building it block by block, brick by brick and you start seeing what works and what's attracting people, what's repelling people. And it's based on you. It's based on your personality and whatever it is within you that you want to do that you want to see come to life that no one else has done, but that you want to see.

You could say The Enoch Wars Books were like that. I wrote books that I just never saw them done in that way. I had ideas for monsters, different spins that I just had never seen before that I wish had been done and that had a spiritual point for them. And not just, "oh let's kill people for the sake of it." It builds up to something over [nine] books and I just never seen that done before in that genre. So, that's my whole point. It comes from something unique within you and you start with that.

STEFANIA: And then that goes into, coaching and other clients they're like, I don't want to have a lair because, or I don't want to do social media or I don't want to do this I don't want to do that, because I'm an introvert and I don't want to have to post 800 times a day. I don't want to have to do these whatever tactics that people are going around who's saying that you need to do. And meanwhile you had one of the most rapid engaged group places, groups, message, reports, however you want to describe it. That was just constant. Thousands of comments a day, even literally just one post would have thousands of comments and it was just insane that you had to have somebody literally summarize it every night, because there's just so much stuff going on. But meanwhile you're like the most introverted person I've ever met.

BEN SETTLE: I wasn't that active in there either. I wasn't really all that active. I ended up shutting it down because I was getting pulled into it too much. But that's the thing, I built a world where other people could interact and most of the engagement was between all of you guys. That one time when you got, at least one, I think it's happened more than once to you. And I know it happened to some other people where you got put in Facebook jail because you were on a date with some schmuck and you were so bored on it that you were rapid posting I think in the Uber or something. I can't remember exactly. And Facebook thought you were a bot.

STEFANIA: I bring this up because like I said, people are often using like, "well I'm an introvert and I don't want to have all this, I don't want to be attached to my computer at the hip. I don't want to have to have all this face time with people. I don't want to have to do …" And there's ways to do that where you're offloaded on, you outsource to other people basically.

BEN SETTLE: Well, who's that chick that you used to read me posts from it and it was comedy for us. The Jetset Babes. That lady hardly ever posted. It was just all the people in there. She just set up an environment, a world she created based around that stuff, which is these chicks trying to find sugar daddies and just let them rabidly go at each other. And she didn't probably have to do much.

STEFANIA: She is a YouTuber who sells these programs and for women to elevate themselves. And by elevate meaning you find someone who's wealthier. And she had a Facebook group called Jetset Babes that she since rebranded because it became very quickly prostitution basically. Basically, the same thing. So, what she would do is she created this area where women can talk to each other about, okay well how about okay, where is this? What should I do, where should I hang out? AKA what hotel bar to hang out with? Which is where it quickly went to prostitution territory and what should they do in order to meet high value men and all this stuff. But it was all these want to be sugar babies interacting with each other and asking each other quick if there was value giving. So, it wasn't strictly a socially type stuff, but it was really rabid engagement there because they're talking about something you can't really talk about elsewhere. You can't without someone calling you a hoe.

BEN SETTLE: And you could say elBenbo' s Lair was very similar. I wasn't a pimp running a prostitution ring. But we did talk about all the stuff that no one 's going to talk about on their main timeline. It gave them permission to just be themselves. And I think this is a very good function of World-Building, is you be that person. And I don't care what you're selling or what market you're in, it doesn't have to even be business related. They can be anything. People are people. The real value doesn't come from the tips. It comes from just interacting with other people and seeing how they think and behave. And sometimes you'll see what not to do. Sometimes you'll see what to do. And I was telling Troy this just last week. there's so much more value, for example, in reading biographies about business people or reading the stories of giant businesses that rise and fall than there is in any "how to" business book.

And it doesn't have to be business, but I'm just saying you'll see more lessons because they're not trying to teach you anything. They're just telling you what happened. And people are people and they make decisions and those decisions have consequences. And sometimes they're good, sometimes they're bad. And that's really where the learning happens. So, what you want is just people interacting, whether they're arguing with each other, whether they're helping each other. It doesn't really matter. My no value thing—I took it to a degree that I probably wouldn't now. I wouldn't do that in most niches. I did it because the internet marketing community is so full of idiots. I couldn't take it any longer. But if I was in Grace's niche for example, and doing dog stuff, I wouldn't forbid value. I would probably encourage it. It's all about the situation, the goal, the reason you build the world. Your reasons will not be the same as mine, and vice versa.

So I would let people interact. That's where you get the gold. People will reveal stuff that they never would talk about publicly. And just because nobody understands them. You're giving people a place to go that's like comic book nerds going to a convention. And I used to be one of them. So, I can tell you it's great to finally have a discussion about my passion without people looking at me like I just grew a third eyeball or something. And that's the value. That really is that engagement with like-minded people that sometimes you're going to deal with trolls and putting them out to pasture is fun for everybody and you have fun. And that fun will trickle down to everybody else. But if it's this really rigid thing, in my experience, even though elBenbo's Lair wasn't that rigid, I had three rules.

It wasn't like there were that many. But those rules of no pitching, no virtue signaling, and no giving value forced people to have personalities. I don't know if this is going to be much of a problem in a non internet marketing type niche, or any niche where you just have a lot of grandstanding, this is where it's going to be a problem. But most niches aren't like that. Most niches are full of regular people. They're not full of these wannabe rock stars like everybody in internet marketing thinks they are. They're all trying to—

STEFANIA: Everybody's profile pictures on stage.

BEN SETTLE: Exactly. They're all on stage and they're all trying to poach people from your group. And that's why I did what I did. But I don't think it's necessary in most cases. Disney had rules. He got savaged by the press when he launched Disneyland because there were so many rules, it wasn't an amusement part like everyone was used to. Apple when they started putting out the iPad and the app store, they had all these rules, they still have rules. And a lot of people think those rules are rigid and I think they are too. But they're also there to protect their users from spam, porn, viruses. And Jobs even got into this debate with a popular technology blogger back then. He actually engaged with this guy one on one.

Imagine the CEO of a billion-dollar company getting into this pissing match with a blogger. But this guy was complaining that Jobs didn't give them a lot of freedom with the apps. And Jobs is like, "I am giving you freedom. I'm giving you freedom from pornography, I'm giving you freedom from spam, I'm giving you freedom from viruses." That's what I'm talking about with rules. It's like they have to be there to protect everybody. But they don't have to be these super rigid 20 point things. Even if you look at SocialLair, if you go to SocialLair.io, you can read the community guidelines. I purposely asked Mike Young, I said, "Look, we got to get this on one page written in plain English, just protect our platform and our interests and protect the interests of our clients." And he did.

And you'll see that it's not really all that bad. As long as you're not acting like a freaking criminal and doing evil stuff, you're fine. And I think that's a good way to look at it. That's how you build worlds. All worlds, if you're going to have a world, you're going to have to have societies. And every society has laws and rules to protect people from each other and also to protect people from themselves. Otherwise, you have chaos, you have anarchy, you have blood in the street. You could have a little of that. But it should still be controlled like elBenbo's Lair was. But elBenbo's Lair was more like the old West. You can go out and duel, and if someone died, just make sure you clean up the mess, otherwise you're going to get fined. But it's your world. You set the rules and enforce the rules however tight or loose as you see fit. I can't tell you what rules to set, and neither can anyone else.

STEFANIA: Yeah, basically the community guidelines for SocialLair is basically just be cool and don't be an asshole. That's the two rules essentially.

BEN SETTLE: And it's funny, I think writing our community guidelines was the project Mike Young had been waiting his whole legal career to do. He got to say things that no other client would let him write probably. And notice that we even have fun at that stage. If it ain't fun for us, it's not going to be fun for you. If it's not fun for you, why the hell would you be around in our world? I mean, you can only get so many tips and guidelines that you couldn't just get on Google if you really wanted to or that you couldn't just pirate on a pirate site. There's something else at play here that you can only get in a social environment. And I say this as an introvert, so that's something to think about.

STEFANIA: So, one of the things also, and you briefly mentioned it a little bit ago, and actually it dovetails into what Danielle was talking about and she followed up in the chat with, and you're right, I don't know if it works or not other than people who seem to create a following or I'm being boring. Even Frank Kern recently did a thing saying this is controversial, but you don't need to post all the time and then tells you to post three times a day.

BEN SETTLE: And there's nothing controversial. Exactly. There is a genius there that people miss because they see the horse shit and all that. But he has created a world. Now it's full of people I wouldn't want in my world, but that doesn't make it any less effective of a world. He's created a persona and a world around himself that even though he's not that active in the game anymore, he still has Twitter bros and every newbie under the sun preaching about and bowing at his altar. And there's something to be said about that. And that should give someone who is an introvert hope.

You just have to direct and guide. You be the puppet master. If you're an introvert, you just be the puppet master. You just guide, set agendas, let the characters do what they're going to do. This goes back to sociological World-Building versus psychological World-Building that I talk about in elBenbo Press. The best epic stories, let's take *Game of Thrones*, the books, not necessarily the show, the ones that were actually written. This is why it was all awkward how it ended. He just built a world, and he threw the characters in there and he just let them do what they would do. I don't think he imposed his will on what everyone had to do. And that's the way I look at it. Just create a world and let people get in there and let them interact and these happy little accidents will happen. And there's something to be said about that.

STEFANIA: One of the things that, and this is something, and not to plug SocialLair, but to plug SocialLair that the platform, not necessarily the book, but one of the things I think that why Frank Kern has his berserkers, if you will, is because he had a very, at least from my understanding, an earlier entrance into the marketplace before all the other gurus joined the guru casino. So, people like-

BEN SETTLE: Ken McCarthy could tell you a lot about that. Because he didn't get Frank started, Frank had his own thing going. But he was saying that he gave him the first serious internet marketing platform where he let him speak at a System Seminar. And you could say the same about a lot of those early guys. I'm not saying Ken's the reason they became big or anything, but the honest ones will say, yeah, he definitely, it's like when I talk about, for example, I talk about Rich Schefren.

He opened a door for me that never could have been opened by anybody else any other way, but he didn't make me or anything. But he opened a door that helped me accelerate things very, very quickly. And I could name about four or five other people who have done the same thing. I think that's also a function of World-Building. You build a world and you attract certain people, including people with more influence than you and you just never know where this stuff's going to go or who's going to be in there. It's transcends you and it transcends marketing. It's something else.

STEFANIA: I told you about this in the Jetset Babes thing. They had a name for men who dangled the carrot for too long that the girls would entertain the guy but they wouldn't get the allowance and the car, whatever the hell they wanted. They called them salty daddies.

BEN SETTLE: And I would've been the margarita salt daddy. I would've been the poster child. They put my picture around there, like they put thug posters up in post offices—stay away from this guy. But that's all I would do. I mean, when did I even buy anything for you? It was months other than a drink at the bar or something. It was ...

STEFANIA: Yeah. Well, I also don't ask for anything.

BEN SETTLE: Even the wedding ring, it's like you picked it out and I said, well okay, it's not too expensive, it was like, what $400? Your mom wanted it to be $30,000.

STEFANIA: Yeah, she wanted me to get the ring that she liked.

BEN SETTLE: I tell you how cheap I really could be and this will make you feel better. Because I've been listening to this audio book called *Slugfest*, which it's my third time through it and I just finished it again today. And it's about the rivalry between DC Comics and Marvel Comics. A lot of corporate espionage. It's a useful book if you're in business. And there's this guy, Perlmutter, bought Marvel comics and he is such a tight wad. This guy was such a tight wad.

He not only ended all the company parties and all that, that's fine, but he actually had signs if they had to use the bathroom and it wasn't just like they had to go number two, they were instructed to go to the McDonald's at the bottom in the building. And that's not even the worst part. He would actually yell at people if they didn't use both sides of the paper if they were using the copy machine. And this guy would eat a dollar and probably shit out a penny. He would stay after hours and go through all their garbage cans and if he saw that they were throwing out too many paperclips and not reusing them, he'd pick them out the garbage can and then leave them on the desk for the next day.

STEFANIA: Oh my God.

BEN SETTLE: Now I'm not that salty. Okay, that's salt daddy right there. That's like taking on a date and reusing the date somehow. It's like, it just, no. It's a whole other—

STEFANIA: Is that why you use the bathroom at the restaurant nearby?

BEN SETTLE: I don't want a higher water bill around here. I go outside. Why should Zoe have all the fun? And that's the world. Sometimes it's not the most sanitary world, but it's a world.

STEFANIA: And it's a cheap world too.

BEN SETTLE: Yes, Nelson. It's called Slugfest and it's by a guy named his last name 's Reed or Tucker I think. I can't remember, but you'll see it. It's about DC and Marvel. You can't miss it. But even better than that book if you're into that stuff, Nelson, it's called *Marvel Comics: The Untold Story.* I've read it four times now. It's so good. It's really one of the best books I've read. Not because it's a business book but because of all the lessons you can mine from it. It's astounding. So, I would start with Marvel comics: The Untold story and then Slugfest, because Slugfest 's not nearly as good. But they're still complimentary books. They're very interesting to read the one after the other. And very good for World-Building.

STEFANIA: So, I did want to touch on this one thing that we talked about a bit earlier in the call and going back to Danielle 's original comment before about people posting boring things. And one thing I think, and you tell me if I'm wrong, which I know you will be more than happy to do, Ben, but I think that some people conflate what engagement really means, or at least they conflate any engagement versus quality engagement. Now one of the things, I am actually reading Social Lair now. I have only 80 pages left. And in it you talk about creating thread holes and creating these, again, these threads where it's thousands upon thousands of comments. I got put into Facebook jail. I know a number of other people did too, just from commenting too much too fast. But it's not just like, oh because we're commenting to some banal post about Coke versus Pepsi. If you remember that checklist.

BEN SETTLE: Oh yeah, that stupid checklist. Yeah, I made fun of that in the book too.

STEFANIA: Yeah. And I picked the fight with her by the way. That was quality engagement. But with the person who created that checklist.

BEN SETTLE: That was very good, Stefania. Absolutely. That's a perfect example.

STEFANIA: Yeah. Well, I don't know, should I go into that?

BEN SETTLE: And I'm not real loose with the compliments with you so you know I mean that, Stefania. But we can go into that. But I just want to say something about all that engagement. You will notice that the real engagement didn't start until probably the 50th comment. At which point it took some weird turn that had nothing to do with the original post. Somebody will say something flippantly or not, maybe they've been drinking, maybe they're just in a good mood.

STEFANIA: More often than not.

BEN SETTLE: Maybe they saw something they didn't like, it had nothing to do, and it turned into something else. And that was where the real engagement came from. Really, I'm just throwing a match out there into the fire pits. But I'm not really the one that stokes up the fire. That's what the people do. So, go ahead and talk about that list. That's a good story. I think it's a very interesting take on things.

STEFANIA: Yeah, so there is this person, it was her and her husband are internet marketing duo type thing and they're really into MLM. So, that should give you an insight into what kind of internet marketing they're into, really smalty, crappy stuff. So, they had this opt in that it was a PDF of top 50 things you can ask your list for instant engagement, that kind of thing. And it was just asking really stupid questions like Coke versus Pepsi or do you sleep with the bedroom door open at night and people will just go on in the comments. Well, I have my door closed and how do you mean? And it's just, it got engagement, because for whatever reason, other than people becoming dopamine fiends, they will just comment on this stuff. But it wasn't the type of engagement that would result in a thread hole.

So, I want to make that really, really clear. It's like there's a thing about people wanting to get eyeballs on their post and getting people to comment and interact with it to beat an algorithm or something versus to actually put out something that one, makes sense. Two, and not even talking about no value type value, but that's something that people actually would be interested in. Other than people typing to hear themselves talk about, well I prefer Diet Pepsi. What else? Do they really care what all the hundred other people care about? They don't.

They stated their opinion and walked away. Basically, it's a flash in the pan type deal. And it's like a post versus having true engagement where people are repeatedly refreshing the thread, interacting over and over again, getting in fights in there. You know what I mean? Having disagreements. There's no disagreement really. I don't think that people are going to be slugging it out in the comments about Coke versus Pepsi. It's a different sort of thing. So, I do think that needs to be clear and maybe you can add even more insight into this, Ben, about why people do that, who cares?

BEN SETTLE: Well, I can tell you it's the equivalent of small talk and small talk isn't engaging. It's forced. Now maybe that's just because I hate small talk with a passion, but small talk only gets you so far. If you have an agenda when you're talking to someone, you can't small talk forever and get much. There's nothing there. If you remember one of our early conversations, we used to argue about immigration.

STEFANIA: Yes.

BEN SETTLE: We didn't small talk. I jumped into it like that, because I wanted to test you. I wanted to see just how bat shit you were after being in the life coach niche. But those were engaging sometimes arguments. And that's engagement. Right now we're having an engaging conversation. It's not just small talk. And the problem with these idiotic checklists is it's just small talk. It's like how's the weather? I'm not going to ask someone how's the weather? I'm going to say, did you hear about that fricking tsunami that came in that wiped out all of Indonesia? I'm going to jump into the deep end so to speak. And that's engagement. But you can't have that with small talk. And I'll tell you one of those things that made me shake my head at how small thinking everybody was.

But is when you'd see people trying to game, because you talk about gaming the algorithms and all that and because Facebook for example, won't let you just sell I guess in your post or they frown on it, people would say, "see the first comment for the link."

And I'm thinking, how dumb is that? Really? Why don't you just talk about something that's related to what you're selling and get a conversation going and then start talking about it. For example, when I had that drag out fight in elBenbo's Lair. I'm not naming names because I honestly don't have anything against her. As you know, she apologized. She apologized, She's fine. Last I heard She's with a really cool guy and everything. She was just going through some hard times, I think, divorced and all that and just whatever. She just did what she did.

But she came in guns blazing. I write about this in the Social Lair book. Guns blazing at me. She came in all out of context. And she didn't understand that there was an atmosphere of just joking around and all that. And the sandwich making jokes, which we're getting dumb at that point, but people were still doing it. But she comes in, "Ben, you're a sexist, misogynist asshole,…" with every ist you could think of. Now, that was engaging. I love her for that though. See, I wasn't mad at all. I was like, "oh, I love this woman!" You know what—if she had been 30 years younger, I might have had to date that one instead of you, Stefania. Passion like that doesn't grow on trees.

STEFANIA: Harrumph!

BEN SETTLE: Okay. I loved her at that moment, because she was engaging. She was doing true engagement. She was doing exactly what I wanted. She wasn't coming in maliciously, but she was coming in passionately.

She literally just felt this rage about me. It was real And it was based on something she thought was real and it was real engagement. And I didn't ever, a single time during that entire 500, I don't know how many freaking comments it turned into and how many posts it turned into. I tried to make it last as long as I could, but it fizzled out after a while I think I burned them all out. But I don't know how many Email Players subscriptions I got out of that. It was a lot. I know I got at least a hundred new opt-ins that week, and people buying Email Players, including her friends, who I would've thought were going to be against me. And I never pitched it. I didn't have to because they heard about me.

Suddenly they're Googling me. Suddenly they're finding my site. Suddenly they're on my list. I don't need to hide a link in a comment and tell people to try to game the AI. Because that's not what they're buying. They're not buying the product. They're buying me. And this is how you got to look at your thing. They are buying you first. You are the first sale. It's not your products. You don't have to do these gamifying things. And these like, "oh, I got to trick the algorithms!" No, you just be someone they want to learn more about and have a world for them to come into to engage with you in.

I'm not saying you never sell, you do sell, but you don't have to do the selling directly in your world. It's like there's places to do that, like your email list and all that, but the world sells them on you. You're just naturally demonstrating your knowledge, your experience, just in your everyday conversation without even trying to give value. You don't have to. Just the way you hold yourself up, your confidence level, all that. That's what does the selling.

I'm not making fun of direct marketers. I am a direct marketer. It took me many years to work this out. I think this is what drives direct marketers nuts. Because you can't track this, you can't test it, you can't scale it. It's something you got to take chances on. You got to make mistakes. It takes time. You need patience. But I'm telling you the payoff, I dare say most of the people on this here right now probably came from me and not Troy I'm guessing. And because they were in my world in some way. Not because of my email list. But that was a part of my world. But you were in my world and you became not just Learnistic members but Profit Pirates clients. To me that's very telling. And so that's something to think about too.

STEFANIA: There you have it.

BEN SETTLE: I'm going to have an aneurysm on this call if I keep this up. I'm getting worked up here.

STEFANIA: I know. I was going to say, you're coming up on 56 minutes.

BEN SETTLE: This is turning into one of our Ravings of an Adman podcasts. This is what this is turning into.

STEFANIA: All right, guys. So, we'll have our next call next month.

BEN SETTLE: Yeah, whatever it is.

STEFANIA: So, until then I'll see you guys in the Lair. All right. Bye.

The Wonderful World of Design Debauchery

Training from the prestigious Profit Pirates coaching program.
www.EmailPlayers.com/pirates

STEFANIA: Let's talk more about your book Markauteur then, since that's coming up.

BEN SETTLE: Well, I would love to talk about my book. I like to turn these calls into infomercials for everything I do. And as far as this book goes, there is some damn good stuff in there that I think since we're talking about people wanting to be authentic and all that stuff and we talked about a lot about this, but just in the book in itself, it is all about this at the end of the day. You were telling me about those shoes that they hurt and you put them on, but people line up around the block to buy them.

STEFANIA: Christian Louboutin. And actually here's something else, people have actually gotten surgery so they can better fit into those shoes. I don't know.

BEN SETTLE: And that's what I'm talking about. And there a big theme of "perfection is a lie." If you see something trying to be perfect, it's a lie. It's an absolute lie. So, if you want to be authentic, you got to be flawed. This is something that Troy and I argue about quite frankly, with design. See, you have to understand something about Troy. He's very much an aesthetic type of guy. He grew up with his mom as an artist. His grandma was an artist, his great-grandma. I think four greats back were artists and master quilters.

So, he just grew up with that. And then his dad was a master craftsman at whatever he did. And so he has both these worlds together. So he looks at my stuff and it almost offends him. In fact, I think it does offend him sometimes. And we'll have these arguments. He said, "Well, no, but look what Apple does. It's all perfectly done. And look how nicely formatted their articles are." I would argue Reddit gets a thousand times more people in engagement, maybe a million times more and it's completely flawed and ugly. And I can't even tell what the hell 's going on when reading Reddit.

STEFANIA: Oh, absolutely. The comments are hard to read. So that goes to my point. It could be beautifully formatted, but I don't want to read that. But I will go on Reddit and go down several hundred comments deep, even though I have no idea what's nested and what, because their whole design is retarded, but I still read them anyway.

BEN SETTLE: And then look at Drudge Report. It doesn't deserve it anymore, but it's the most widely, as far as I know, read news site and aggregator. And that site design has not changed at all since 1997, I'm not even exaggerating. It looks like something I would design with the old Netscape Composer. Completely imperfect, the way the three columns and the way it refreshes itself every two minutes or whatever, so you lose your spot on the page or even what headline you're reading. All this stuff logically, should not work. And the beautiful, perfect thing should work logically, but it doesn't. And I know there 're exceptions to this, so I'm not going to say there aren't. But for the most part, I'm hoping that when people walk away from reading my book Markauteur, that they will have a whole new outlook on what's possible because these are some insights that I have gotten over 20 years that have just made it so that I don't have any competition.

There's nobody out there doing the covers I do, the kind of websites I do. Even if you look at the joint stuff I do with Troy, it's not a hundred percent Troy. It's not a hundred percent me either. It's a little bit of both, but those imperfections are built in and there's a reason for that. It stands out. It gets attention. It's a known thing among certain art gallery dealers that the crooked painting is going to be noticed and more likely probably to be bought. It's not logical. It's not supposed to be logical. It's not being logical, or making sense is why I think it works. And once you embrace that, whatever it is that you like doing, and you just start doing what you think is cool and interesting, everything changes. And we are all influenced by other things. Well, nobody else thinks that's cool. And we might even think we're being authentic, but we're still looking at something else.

Kia and I had this discussion. Everybody in the Dan Kennedy world is low brow. That's what everybody does because supposedly that's what works best. Well, I can tell you, these are people who have never tried doing anything on their own and they're just parroting what other people are doing because they don't want to be the one Dan Kennedy fanboy that's trying to do something different. This is actually a huge testament to what he's done, because he's got that following. But I had this when I switched the book people get with Email Players from a spiral bound 8.5 x 11 manual, because I thought that's what you were supposed to do. And I never thought it was cool. I always thought it looked like ass, but whatever. I did it anyway, when I switched it to the format it is now, small type where I have some people are telling me they can't read it.

They're older and they can't read it. One Dan Kennedy fanboy said, "Ben, you ruined the whole value of the book", just a few years ago.

STEFANIA: I remember that.

BEN SETTLE: He said, "All the value is gone because you did this. I consulted with Dan Kennedy and he showed me that if I made it just a binder stuffed with pages and my sales went up 300%." And I'm like, "You are an idiot." He was an Email Players subscriber, but obviously not anymore. And he doesn't even understand the context of what he's learning and it's the context of that whole "let's make everything ugly." You know what people don't understand about that, Stefania?

STEFANIA: Tell the class, please.

BEN SETTLE: And I know this because I read this in one of his old No BS newsletters. So this was many years ago. I wrote articles for one of his business partners. And they handed me all these old, No BS newsletters and said, "turn these into articles." So I read this, it's been in my mind ever since. Because he did the Guthy-Renker infomercials and they did something for Think and Grow Rich. It was some biz opp type thing I think, that obviously targeted the blue-collar crowd. And they did it all pretty and it looked nice and all that, and they got overrun with refunds. So, they decided to make it ugly and low brow, binder stuffed with pages, probably.

And then the refunds pretty much vanished. And he was like "The reason why…" And I don't know if he was guessing this or if it was because they actually did research. I have no idea, but it made sense what he said. He says, "Because people are conditioned to look at something that looks like mass advertising, mass produced books and stuff. They should only be paying $10 or $12 bucks for it at Barnes & Noble and not $200 for it." And there's absolutely a point to that. There's no question about it. However, I don't sell to those people. I'm literally selling $300 to $400 products to businesses, not blue-collar biz opp zombies. They're not looking at any of that stuff. And so one of the reasons I went to perfect bound was just to spite these idiots who all have been trying to take shots at me for years over this. "That won't work, you can't do that. This is stupid. What a dumb... You're wasting your time." Well, I've heard it all. I literally have heard it all.

I just keep putting more and more expensive books out there and I just keep making more and more sales. And I did it just to spite these idiots, I did it to not get their approval. I did it to get their disapproval. And I think this is a big part of it. Don't seek anybody's approval, not mine or anyone else. Seek our disapproval. Try to get disapproval. Now does it mean it's going to work every time? No. Sometimes it'll blow up on you, but I can tell you this, you're going to have a lot more home runs than you would've if you didn't by swinging from the fences like that. And this is a big part of my book Markauteur I'm doing.

I think I say it so many times that I even start saying, "I know you're tired of hearing this, but I'm going to say it again—don't be even 1% me, be 100% you." Whatever that looks like in your design, in your products. I don't care what the format is. Yesterday, one of the two Sarahs here, I don't know which one it is. Nobody knows the difference between you two. That's why we call you the Sarahmese twins. But one of them said something very interesting about marketing using cassette tapes, delivering content. And I thought that was a really cool idea. She's thinking the right way. That's interesting. That's inherently different. And every guru fanboy would say that's a bad idea, don't do it. I don't know, Sarah. I think you should run with testing that idea and seeing what happens. I thought that was a brilliant idea. And I'm giving you props publicly for that. So anyways, I don't know where I'm going with all this, other than just tell these people who don't like your stuff. "Good. Don't look at it."

STEFANIA: So here's something we talked about. I think it was yesterday or the day before, so you as an introvert, you're going against everyone saying, "Oh, introverts, feel better when they're acting extroverted." But part of that also, and this is also part of the book, which is...

BEN SETTLE: I feel really good being a recluse. I don't know why these guys feel better acting like extroverts.

STEFANIA: Well, so here's what I was going to say, that you are really comfortable and just doing this shit that you like. And here's the problem though. And this is also again, I would say it's actually balanced between extroverts and introverts, but for different reasons of that, a lot of people, if not, most people don't actually know what they genuinely like. If people aren't looking and people aren't looking at their Facebook page likes, like the Spotify thing, how Spotify's trying to be a social media platform, it shows you like, "These are your top songs for 2021." And they give you these little images to put it on social media. "Look how different and cool I am and how indie I am for all these random bands that I like that no one's ever heard of. But I'm so cool. I've heard of them."

BEN SETTLE: They all want to show how advanced they are. Something that was on the side B of a cassette tape in 1984 that no one's ever heard

STEFANIA: All that stuff. So, if no one's looking. It's like the world has turned its back on you. No one's paying attention to you. What actually do you like to do? You're like, "Well, I'm just going to go back to my office and watch more Subspecies movies." That's what you're going to do.

BEN SETTLE: Absolutely. And that's how I approach this. I don't know. I sent this to you to find that, I know I sent this to you and I quoted it somewhere in the book. One of my customers, he got Brand Barbarian. This is just a month ago. He got Brand Barbarian and he told me his wife said, "This guy, Settle. I think there's something wrong with him. His covers are so dark and gloomy. Don't tell him I said that or he is going to cuss me out in an email!" First of all, I would never do that. I love this person. I want more people like that, to be honest with what they think. And my whole thought was she secretly likes all these dark and gloomy covers, but she can't admit it.

She's not allowed to by society's standards. And I use the example of the scene in Pulp Fiction where the guy gets shot in the back seat. It's horrifying and disturbing, but it's funny. But I don't really want to laugh out loud in front of other people necessarily when that happens. It's like disturbingly funny. And so I look at it like that. So besides you, I'm guessing only one, maybe two people on this call will know the name I'm about to drop. Lauren definitely knows who this person is. I don't know if anyone else does. And I'm talking about the comic book artist, the one and only the, I don't want to say esteemed... but I've always loved this guy's artwork. Rob Liefeld. All right. This guy does everything wrong. Everything. He literally draws two right feet on a character. Everything's out of a proportion. Everything's crazy. He literally had writers quit on him. Louise Simonson on the New Mutants title couldn't take it anymore because Rob would draw this insane stuff where the interior of a building shows round windows, but the outside showed a square window. And art directors used to have fights about this guy, but his editor would not change anything because his stuff was bringing in so many new readers, probably like me.

I always say, if you look at any of my products, any of my books, my writing, anything, it's just one giant Rob Liefeld drawing. And there are people who like that and there are people who hate it, but it's surprising how many people hate something like that who secretly like it. But they don't think they're supposed to like it. And none of their friends like it. So they can't admit they like it. But deep down in the deepest recesses of their minds and opinions, they like it. And that's why they keep coming back for more, even if it's just to troll and hate on something.

STEFANIA: So, my theory has been that the reason why people don't know what it is that they like or not in touch with that or not just going with whatever they think is cool. And it's not just what you think is cool because I'm sure after the book comes out, there's going to be people like, well I have to have more horror in my stuff. I need to be—

BEN SETTLE: And that's the wrong approach to have. I hope anyone who gets this book reads the interview with you in it, as it's probably one of those valuable parts of the book.

STEFANIA: You're only saying that because I'm on the phone with you.

BEN SETTLE: I've been editing this damn thing. And we talked about your favorite artist, Egon, whatever the hell...

STEFANIA: Egon Schiele.

BEN SETTLE: Right. Nobody in their right mind is going to say, "That's my favorite artist", but you. I looked at it, I'm like, "This is just looks like fun house mirror Gollum or something." I'm sitting there looking at it because I'm like, "Huh." And the guy's crazy prostitute drawings are starting to grow on me... like mold. But that's the thing. It's fun to talk to someone who has truly authentic taste. Even if I'm like, "I don't get that." I can have a discussion with that person. I'm probably going to be more likely to buy something from that person because they're being honest with me and they're showing me some weird flaws here. But there's something about that. And you can't fake it. You can't fake it. You almost have to purposely go out there and show the world that, "No, I really do like this thing that everybody else thinks is stupid or dorky or whatever." And not only not apologize for it, but actually brag about it.

It's almost like a version of making the skeleton dance. And when you do that, and then you do that with your design side of your business, everything 's going to change and it's not about, "Oh, this is what Ben does." And that's the worst thing you could do. Now one of the interviews in there's with Keith Commins. He does all my website stuff. You guys don't know about this. There's a reason why I hire this guy for everything. Now I'm telling you, I've had people tell me, "Oh, that's not that great. It's amateur." No, he always does everything I ask, but he puts his own flare on things and he understands what makes direct response work. So, he and I work very well together.

Me and Keith work. We have an ebb and flow. And I can tell you something about Keith that you guys probably don't know. And I asked him this very specifically when I interviewed him for Markauteur, and I didn't even know what he was going to say when I asked it to him, I just had this gut feeling. And that is this guy, for fun is right now, he lives in Barcelona.

He's been living there for a few years. His idea of fun is going around with this camera and just looking at architecture and taking pictures of weird shots of buildings. Now that in itself is not all that special. But when I asked him this, I go, "well, does this influence what you do in web design?" And he had never been asked that before.

He never thought about it before, but when he thought about it, he is like, actually yes, he goes, "It doesn't do it directly." But there are times when he can see direct examples when he's been influenced by a piece of architecture. I forget the guy's name. There's a very popular architect out there that did most of the buildings he likes and it shows. So, when he does some design for me or his other clients, not trying to impress anybody at all, he's not even trying to impress the client. He's just doing what comes out of his soul when he's designing. Now he doesn't look at it as an art thing probably. But I can tell you as someone who's hired him many times for many different projects, he's doing my new opt-in page now, which is like Rob Liefeld on steroids.

See, I think it looks cool. So, I don't care if anyone else likes it. And I guarantee you it'll perform better than the one I have now. And we talked about this, and I said, it'd probably be good for everyone to just go spend some time who wants to learn how to think about design, to just go to a museum and just see what interests you. And it can't be, "Oh, well, everyone else likes that exhibit." No, it's got to be that thing that you like. And it could be the weirdest thing in the museum. All right. You may be really creepy and into art like the Virgin Mary with urine on it and all that. And if that's the case I don't want anything to do with you.

But let's say you're a normal human. Now, Stefania, you're always limited by the drop and drag software that you use with ClickFunnels. You're limited by that. There's only so much you could do, but I bet, and I'm going to have you do this eventually. When you want to relaunch all your stuff… this is going to be a gift to you. I'm going to get a Keith Commins gift card for you. I want him to do your stuff. And I want you to have a long two hour discussion with him and he builds you something that's a hundred percent you and I guarantee you There'll be some of that Egon stuff in it.

It doesn't mean you're going to draw yourself in a weird pose and all that, but it'll be in there, the strands of DNA of what you are absolutely into on that you just like for whatever reason you think it's cool, it'll show up. And it'll be very interesting. And I think everybody listening, whether you do your own stuff or you hire someone to do it, just do that, go find something that just you think is cool artistically and redesign your opt-in page based on that. Not make it look like it, but just be influenced by it and really think about it. Talk to a designer, talk to Keith, hire Keith. I don't get a kickback if you hire him, in fact, you hire him, you're going to slow down his progress on my stuff.

But trust me, if you can just step outside of yourself so to speak a little bit, and look down on you as if you're a different person and you're observing yourself and what you really are into design wise and artistically wise, have that discussion with someone like Keith or a Kia Arian or whoever you like to use, or you can do it yourself too. But I think you'll find that by collaborating with someone it's going to be better. And in my experience at least. Just watch what happens. I guarantee you'll have the most unique looking opt-in page. It may even pull better, but you never know. Probably you're going to get a better quality customer, better quality lead. You're probably going to turn away people you don't want. All this stuff comes together if you're just honest and you just tell the truth. That's my thought, Stefania.

STEFANIA: I think actually, and this is especially for fellow extroverts, because I've had to do this. And you could say that you, Ben, gave me permission to be this way, which is if There's something that you think is cool, and whether it's like, you're just rolling around Pinterest or just Google Images or just walking around or whatever. I wouldn't go with the first thing that comes to mind or go with the first, "Okay. That's it?" No. Go a few layers deeper than that. Whether it's a few more scrolls or a few more minutes into it, because you're going to start taking that outside voice out, starting to lower the volume until it hits mute, if you will.

And if it's something that you're like, no, I can't do that. No, that's the one that you need to do. And I mentioned this to you this morning, that there were so many times whether it's like we said at the top of the call, professionally speaking or things I had to do, there were so many times that I either dressed a certain way or I listened to certain music or I did certain things because that was what the external image that I created for myself. That is what people expected of me.

BEN SETTLE: How much happier are you right now? I know I could say that I had you doing it, but technically you do whatever you want, but I'm like, here's what I like. And you want to make me happy and all that, but you're very comfortable in the Pacific Northwest redneck look.

STEFANIA: When I met you, I was wearing four-inch heels, two inches of makeup on and super tight dresses. And I was always dressed to the nines and it's just uncomfortable after a while. And I didn't realize this just being in your own skin. So, I know that sounds like find yourself. And actually, I said it to you directly was that a lot of people, I feel like in their need to "find themselves" and discover their authentic self really is just finding the shit that you like and just going with it.

BEN SETTLE: Well, here's something to think about. Now, this is also out of the book, but I totally got this from Eugene Schwartz's Breakthrough Advertising. He doesn't talk about it from design specifically, but it's there.

So when you do, when we're talking about here, all the stuff we just talked about with your opt-in page and go into a museum and finding out what it is that you just really do like. And maybe the thing that I'd be embarrassed to tell everyone I like, because that's fine.

So, here's the thing, when you do all this stuff and I started from scratch I had negative influence when I got in this business. All right. I can tell you right now, when you do that, you will start tapping into that same thing. Whatever that thing, Stefania, of the guy's shoes that people are just identifying with that shoe. It could be Air Jordans, quite frankly, it's the same effect. The people identify with this thing. They got to have it. It's part of their personality. You become a part of your customer's personalities. It's like, they're not even comfortable unless you're in their life somehow. I'm telling you it's a real phenomenon. I'm the same. We're all like this, by the way, we're all like this to some degree.

I first admit I am to certain things. We identify certain things with our personalities and lives because it taps into that thing and won't be logical or make sense. And that's why I think it works so well. Because if you tried to think through it, it wouldn't work. You can't plan this. You can't strategize it, but you can aim it. You just can't create it. You just have to do certain things and it happens. What it all comes down to is when you do this, you're starting the process of World-Building because you're building something, that's building your own Narnia, quite frankly, and you're building a doorway and I know this is all weird and it is, this is why it's very hard to explain. I would say 20 to 30 minutes of my two-hour discussion with Kia Arian in Markauteur in the interview section was just trying to talk through this.

It's hard to verbalize this, but it's the beginning of your World-Building in your business. It's certainly a doorway into your world. It's a wardrobe. It's like they walked into this, they've seen this interesting wardrobe that looks different and they walk in and suddenly they're walking on snow and they see a lamp post, "Whoa, where the hell am I?" This is the goal. And it all starts with what you think is cool and what comes out. And I want to be very clear about this. You still have to sell things people want. This is not the offer side. I'm talking about the design side.

You can't do this artsy-side with your offers. You could, but you would have to be really on a whole other level that I'm certainly not at maybe, but it starts with that thing. And some people manufacture this like they hire a Kardashian to promote their stuff or whatever, but we don't all have that luxury. So all we can do is use our wits. And this is where I think it all begins. I really do. I think World-Building when it comes to design, it begins with finding that thing that you just like, and you think is cool design-wise and it all starts with that I think.

The One World of Power

Training from the prestigious Profit Pirates coaching program
www.EmailPlayers.com/pirates

TROY BROUSSARD: All right, welcome, everybody, and welcome back. This is going to be fun, we're going to do some stuff a little different. Ben, one of the things that really interests me about how you write is the way that you're both a copywriter, but also a novelist. You enjoy that creative storytelling novel creation aspect, and I know you're a big comic book fan and have all this culture in that area, and I know that you've taught quite a bit about World-Building. But this is a concept for an engineer like me that's a little bit foreign, and We've had a lot of talks back and forth on it, but I'd love you to just tell us what World-Building is first of all.

BEN SETTLE: Okay. So, before I get into the what's and the how's, I want to give some context. I didn't realize this until about many years ago when I wrote my first novel, and I got this email from this woman on my list who her business is they set writers up with editors, so like an agent, but they don't set people up with publishers or anything like that. She goes, "I don't really like your daily emails, but I read your *Zombie Cop* and you're really good at World-Building. I'd love to just set you up with an editor, I don't get paid for anything." She was just a fan of it.

I didn't really think much of it, because I was self-publishing, I wanted to keep it that way. But I started realizing I've been doing that in my marketing ever since I got into business. It was just a natural thing, it's natural not because of some inborn genius or anything like that, but it's because I spent my childhood doing two things. One, living in my own head. I was a very introverted kid, I don't know, I would rather just sit there and map out entire storylines in my mind than hang out with people at parties or whatever. It's just what I did. As a small child I played with toys, but I wouldn't just play with my toys, I would create entire adventures with my toys and the people, with storylines. My brain just worked that way. Couple that with playing a lot of Dungeons & Dragons, all the time, whoever I could get to play with me, my friends, my brother, his friends. I just was obsessed with it, I was one of these guys who was obsessed with just role playing, not even just Dungeons & Dragons, but all these other ones too, there's so many out there. Anyone who is interested in that, I highly recommend the biography of Gary Gygax, I forget the guy who wrote, his name, it's called Empire of Imagination. And it was really fascinating reading that, seeing the mind of this guy.

But Gary Gygax is the guy who created modern-day role-playing games as we know it, and you wouldn't even see things like *Game of Thrones* without him, and *Dune* and all these other popular games, *World of Warcraft*, etc. So, there's a context there, it's not something that I can say, "Just do this, this and this," with a checklist. That's why I think, even though you and I talk about it all the time, it's like you're trying to explain mobile apps to me. It took months for me, and I think that's how it is with you with this, because it's just not how your brain works, but it is something that people can learn and do.

It became very apparent to me that I was doing this, especially when I started emailing every day and I started creating my own world. It goes beyond writing style, I actually create a world with depth and characters. Everyone right now, Troy, you are a character in my world. Stefania is a character in my world. My dog is a character in my world. I populate it with characters and we interact and there's storylines and things happen, I write emails about them. I took this to a ridiculous degree and this is where I did start consciously doing it, at the end of 2016 I had this Facebook group that was just like all the other Facebook groups, just all your how-to marketing, this and that, everybody sharing value and whatever.

Then one night I was sitting at this bar up in Florence, and for some reason I just asked some stupid question out of the blue in there. I said, "Who can guess what kind of beer I'm drinking right now?" I got all these people, I didn't think anybody would give a crap, quite frankly, I was just bored. But the answers from everybody were so ravenous and people felt like they really knew me. They were trying to guess based on what they knew of my personality and my business, because that's the kind of world I built. Fast forward another week or two, and I started doing this on purpose. I started purposely building a world thinking about my biggest influences for World-Building, which were Dungeons & Dragons, the late TV producer Aaron Spelling, who did a lot of teeny-bopper type soap opera shows, but he was really good at building worlds in his shows and things like that.

I started adding depth to my group—rules, laws, things you can and can't do, who can do certain things and who can't. I had a hierarchy of women, which took a huge life of its own, let me tell you. That was actually very hair-raising. I had an inner circle of people who I would allow to give value in there, nobody else could. I had my own border wall, before Trump 's wall. I had my wall where I would not let certain people join. I wouldn't let them join, for example, if they were in too many other groups. Because at the time, I don't know how it is now, I haven't been on Facebook in a while, but back then as a group owner, if somebody tries to join it says how many other groups they are in. So if it said 400 or something ridiculous, I didn't want them in mine. I'm not just going to be one of that many fricking groups, they're going to pay attention or go away. So, I started instituting all of these rules.

And by the way, I say all this not so people will just do the same thing, but to think like a world builder. Think like a Tolkien did or a C.S. Lewis. These guys are world builders, they're sociological storytellers, not psychological storytellers. I'll just end my little bit here on this, There's a difference between the two. Sociology is the building of societies. Sociological storytelling is where you just create this world and you create the situation, you create the characters and you let them run free. The story is not relying on anyone living or dying, you don't direct the plot, you let it unfold based on what the characters are doing, their decisions.

If you watch the Game of Thrones show, Games of Thrones fans know what I'm talking about here when they were following the books, not when the showrunners started making things up. But I'll try to make it accessible to everybody. The author of the books is really slow, so the show got ahead of where the books were. Now, when they were following the books, it was a very sociologically built show, that's why you'd have characters dying left and right. You're like, "What the hell? That was a main character!" No, but not really, because it's about the structure of the story, not about what individual people are doing. You're not forcing characters to do anything. As opposed to most stories, which is psychological storytelling. Pretty much any Hollywood movie is psychological storytelling. The writers are manipulating the characters to do certain things and creating circumstances just so a character will do a certain thing to get to the ending they want.

Nothing right or wrong about either one of them, but when you saw the Game of Thrones show, when it started getting dumb, it's because they were psychological storytellers trying to fit it into a sociological built world, and it looked stupid. The whole last season was just insanely dumb, it was stupid, it really let everyone down. Made it so they aren't re-watchable, which just kills backend sales. Well, take this to business. In the business world, if you create a sociologically built business, you're not relying just on metrics. Psychologically built businesses, like what you see everyone do in direct marketing, ask them what they want, obsess over so-called "what's working now", test and track every tiny little metric no matter how pointless, and base offers on surveys, which I know you're a big fan of, Troy. I say that as a joke, by the way. Troy hates them just as much as I do.

So it's psychological, and you can build a very successful business that way, but you're not going to build a Disney or an Apple doing that. It's got to have its own culture, its own world. Look at Apple versus Microsoft. Apple, at least when Steve Jobs was running the thing, it was its own culture, its own world, very distinct, you couldn't copy it or knock it off. It was very sociologically built. In fact, that quote I shared with you, Troy, that you like so much, when they launched the Apple II or whatever, I think it was the Apple II. And it did really well and a reporter asked Steve Jobs, "What kind of focus groups did you do with this? Who did you ask for who would want this?"

He goes, "I didn't ask anyone, did Alexander Bell ask anyone who wanted the phone?" So, to sum up, I think Stefania figured it out best she noticed I had people fighting each other in there on purpose, I would create posts and let people just fight each other over it, without even saying anything. Then when they got bored, if I didn't do that, if I didn't throw some red meat out there, I would point them to somewhere off my group and make fun of somebody or whatever, and then they would all go attack him.

She goes, "Your group's like a Vikings 'den, people just sitting around sharpening their weapons, getting into drunken fights, and when they aren't fighting each other they go out and attack someone else." Then she would compare it to other groups out there, and say, "Well, this group is more like a sales conference, that's boring. This group is like just a pub, very boring." I think that to me was a very good analogy. I built an actual world out of my group, it wasn't just a themed group where people share value and all that. It was a world. I wasn't even allowing value to be shared in there, that was forbidden, forcing people to have to think and have personalities. And it was insanely addictive. My emails are the same way, my business is the same way.

If you look at my books, my suite of books, they're all characters in a world that I've built, my own world. So I hope that helps make sense of things.

TROY BROUSSARD: So just to clarify, because I know, I don't want people to take it literally like that you were starting fights and sending people out to fight with others and all that. What you really mean is just creating heated debates and very opinionated controversial statements that get a lot of massive engagement and appeal to people's visceral response, where they don't even filter their responses, they come across unfiltered and just let it roll. So it was stimulating a lot of engagement at the visceral level. So give me an example of how you might do that, or just give me an example in the past of how you might have done that in the group that you had.

BEN SETTLE: Sometimes I would literally pick fights, because I was just having fun in there and I just wanted to challenge people's thinking. I'm a big fan of giving people options for thinking differently. So they didn't have to agree with me, but it was weird how rabid it would get, and I was creating these rabid fanboys and fangirls. Where if I just merely suggested, or if I just posted a link to someone else's Facebook page or a post they did outside of the group, they would descend on these people, to the point, I had no control over it. I didn't even tell them to go do anything, I'm just saying, "Look at this." Maybe I'd make a smart-ass comment or something.

Suddenly, these people are getting overrun with all these people and it all got traced back to me, and people were trying to threaten me and that sort of thing. In one case, just to show you how rabid this gets, there was this copywriter, I'm not going to name her, because her and I have since then, we get along fine now, she was just going through some personal stuff, she said, and she just acted inappropriately. Where she came in and I gave people, like you said, I gave people permission to be themselves. By the way, this was a huge thing. People knew they could go on there and be themselves and I wasn't going to censor them, within limits. I had to have a moderator to get rid of the really stupid crap people would post in there, but as long as they weren't sharing value or virtue signaling, they were letting people get to know them and get to know me and it was a very, very intimate place like that.

I knew things about people in there their best friends and families don't know about them, it was really like that. It got even to the point where people would call it real life, and anything outside of my group was fake life. You know how Facebook is, you're in a group so you see all the group posts, if you have your timeline set like that, well, there was so many concurrent posts going on in my group with two or three or four or 500 plus comments. I used to call them a thread-hole, because they would just take these weird turns that had nothing to do with the post eventually. People would post on their main timeline thinking they were in my group, saying something they probably didn't want the rest of their friends to know. They'd be embarrassed about it, but that's how it was getting. They could just be themselves.

I can only take so much of it, because I'm a private guy and all that, and eventually it just got to be too hair-raising for me and I just got out of it. It's all about engagement, that's all it was, was engagement. It was hyper engagement. I was telling you that if I was a coach or a consultant or freelancer, I guesstimate, I'll never know, but I guesstimate that I would have made an extra two, three, four or $500,000 in there easily. People are buying my stuff just to be further in my world as an Email Players subscriber and that sort of thing.

But back to the one chick, I got off track there. So, the chick comes in and

She's read one of my posts about, some kind of misogynist post, you know how I screw around and joke around, and she comes in taking it all seriously, threatening me. I'm like, "Oh, I love this woman!" I said that, I just kept messing with her a little bit. Eventually, she really got angry and another girl stepped in, I'm trying not to name names here, another girl stepped in to defend me, which I didn't really need it, but she wanted to do it, because that's just the reaction people... I had my own Vikings 'den.

One thing led to another and the girl who attacked me, one of her friends tried to defend her, which is perfectly fine with me. But then everyone started attacking that girl, and I didn't even know this until a year later, she told me because we met at a conference actually, she goes, "Yeah, I was getting death threats or threats by phone," may or may not have been actual death threats, I don't know if she was exaggerating, but certainly menacing calls and voicemails, "from people in that group." So that's how far it went, that's why it was getting a little hair-raising for me. I couldn't control it, it became its own thing, which is the point of all this.

It is massive engagement, it is hyper engagement. Once you understand the formula that conflict equals engagement, and let that guide you in World-Building, you cannot not have engagement if you do it right. But it takes a thick skin, you've got to be able to do certain things and go against the grain, like I did. That's where I'm going with that. But mostly I wasn't going out picking on people, although once in a while I would absolutely go pick fights just to get people riled up. One time, and I would do it before I went to bed at night, so for example, just to get massive engagement and just get people riled up, I didn't think, "Oh, I need engagement." I just wanted to get people riled up, I wanted to start a storyline. I just called them storylines.

I got this testimonial from someone and the topic was abortion. So that's naturally a lightning rod topic, and he basically said, "Ben, you changed my mind on this topic when you said the safest place for a baby should be the womb." I just put that in there as a testimonial, knowing full well that was like dropping a bomb in the water. Of course, when I woke up the next morning six, seven hours later, I think there were like five or 600 responses. Everybody fighting each other left and right, people fighting me, a few people agreeing with me. It was amazing. It's not like anyone stopped being a customer of mine. If anything, even the people that disagreed with me, they appreciated the ability to talk about this in a way, where we kept it all civil for the most part. And people who didn't, we just had to silence them. But as long as they weren't insulting each other it was fine.

It was an actual conversation, it was engaging, there was definitely conflict, but it was interesting. I did the same thing with the topic of fat shaming once. I did this post about why shaming is good, and fat shaming is really good, and I gave my reasons. I woke up the next morning and there were five, 600 responses. These are just two of probably dozens of examples of this. But the thing is, and there's this guy that was in there, his name 's Sean, and him and I would disagree a lot on things, but we were very civil with each other. I remember him saying, "Ben, this is an amazing thing you've created here, because it's plumbing the depths of human psychology."

You don't have to go on and talk about these hot fire topics, it can be about anything. In fact, if you try to copy me, you're just going to look like a Tolkien wannabe when they try to compete with Lord of the Rings, or someone who's trying to be a Stephen King and they just come off as a wannabe Stephen King. You want to build your own world about the things that are interesting to you, around your preferences and personality and interests, it can be business, it doesn't have to be business, it can be your rules. That's the whole point, they're your rules, it's your world, your domain and you can do whatever you want with it.

People like that. There will be people who hate it and there will be people who love it, the people who love it, even if they don't like everything that goes on there, they won't be able to look away. So I remember a whole bunch of these groups popping up that were trying to be like me, totally missing the point. They would institute a no-value rule like I did and they totally missed the point. And nobody cared to be in their stupid group, because they missed the entire point. The point is not to create a group or any kind of society World-Building in your business that just, "Oh, here's what Ben said to do." No, you have to understand these things are based on my intolerance for people, my intolerance for nonsense, and all kinds of things that have nothing to do with the average person watching them.

It's got to be about you and your values and your culture and what you want to put in there. Some people will love it, some people will hate it. Just like Apple computers, some people can't stand them, a lot of people love them. I was telling you, Troy, about how there's a reason why back in 2011, where some neuroscientist did brain scans of Apple computer fans and he realized that Apple fans 'brains react when they see an Apple gadget the way a religious person 's brain reacts to their chosen deity. So that's World-Building at its highest level in a corporate setting, and it ain't on accident. This does not have to be on social media. Social can be a part of it, so can your email list, your customer list, your podcast audience—your world is not constrained by a media.

But back to Steve Jobs—it's because Steve Jobs instilled his own culture, his own world, it's his own world. Disney 's the same way, it's its own world, they even have Disney World, it's its own world. Look at Nintendo, they've created their own world with their own characters. Not just like, "Oh, I've got to create characters." No, it's a culture, it's a world, it's a flavor, it's a brand, it feels unique, something unique and fun, or interesting, and so it is. This is a very big topic to talk about. But I'm trying to distill it down as much as I can. There's a lot to it. So, I hope this helps.

TROY BROUSSARD: So, to wrap this up, what would you say would be the first step in this process? To me, you gave us some guidelines there, and I know there's no checklist type thing, but you talked about creating your own characters, creating your own rules, so to me it seems like it's very self-reflective, is your first step of just what you really want to create and what values that you deem to be important in your world. Is that a good first step for someone?

BEN SETTLE: That could be a good first step. If we're going to apply this to business, it's all about looking at every part of your business as another adventure unto itself. Every email sequence selling something is its own role-playing campaign, if that makes sense. It probably would help actually for people to play a role-playing game. It doesn't matter which one. But that would be my suggestion to find a role-playing game, RPG, not a computer one, but an actual one where you sit around with some people and you're rolling dice. I don't care which one it is, and you have someone who's a dungeon master type and you have a module that's already been pre-written and you just go through it as characters.

And then you just start to think, "How would this apply to my business, this structure?" Not the actual game itself, but just this way of thinking. Because I think it really does start there. That's probably why you had a hard time wrapping your mind around it, because you probably just never played these games. You've probably never really written any novels or anything like that, so it's just not as ingrained in you. But I think if we have an event, we should have a session where we all just play Dungeons & Dragons for one of the nights, and just really get people in this World-Building mode and this way of thinking where there's depth to everything.

It's not just a book or a course or whatever, it's got way more depth than that. It's got its own nuances, it has its own flaws, it has its strengths. You look at every customer as a different unique entity, not just a number. Where do they fit in this and what can you do for this person, and how do these characters—these offers—fit into their lives, and how can they benefit from them? Maybe I would have this or I'd offer that. Like I said, it's not really something that can be done with a checklist, it really is changing the way someone thinks. Not changing it like you have to change who you are or anything, but you're just tapping a different side of your brain that starts with storytelling. But it goes way beyond that. It's literally building your own world.

I would say another thing someone could do is watch all the first 10 years of Marvel movies. I don't know, I haven't watched many of the ones after that, because they all started getting too woke for me. But they did a great job building the world. That was a pre-created world, Stan Lee created it for them, you might really want to go look at all the early Marvel comics, see how there was this whole world Stan Lee was building, the characters interacted with each other. In my Facebook group I actually said, "We are trading with this other group." I would get discounts for my people, someone else's group they're running, and vice versa, because I'm thinking more deep than just, "Oh, joint venture."

No, I'm thinking we're doing trade. My people are trading with their people, and it's just a different way of thinking. I would say that's your first step. I even sent all the women in my group to participate in another group's dating pool. Any single chick had to post their profile or I'd kick them out. Just for fun. Wanted them to see the schlubs out there, compared to the guys in my world.

Probably a good thing to watch, actually it's a trilogy of movies, and I don't know what the official trilogy name is, but it starts with the movie *Unbreakable* and then *Split* and then *Glass*. M Night Shyamalan did great World-Building with these three movies. He did by himself what it took Marvel, Disney, DC Comics and all them, Warner Bros to do with 80 years of intellectual property, he did with his own brain, to a smaller extent. But you'll see there's World-Building going on, it's a totally different way of looking at things. You have connectivity going on. Very important. Things in a world connect— sometimes obvious ways, sometimes in non-obvious ways. But everything belongs, and everyone who does belong you'll know. If they don't belong, you'll know. It's something you get a feel for. Birds of a feather really do flock together. All this takes thinking. People will want to ask questions, and just asking questions means they are missing the point and should go through all this again. It's not a checklist. It's not a "do this, and this, and this."

It starts with just thinking like that, and not even worrying about the business part, but just how can you think more like a world builder and less like just a straight marketer? It's something that once you get used to it and you start doing it and thinking about it, it just changes everything you look at. It will certainly apply to your business too. I'm going to add something else to this, Troy, now that I'm thinking about it, because I mentioned We've been doing this at Learnistic, but probably more accurate is I've been doing it at Learnistic, because you've been busy off doing the developing and dealing with the team and all that, and I've just been sitting there thinking about how to create a world, make Learnistic its own world and all that.

It started with when I started writing the email, I sat there for 20 days and I wrote 100 and some emails, I wrote the sales page and all that really methodically. I even add World-Building in there as a benefit, even though a lot of people won't understand it, but I could explain it in a way that I think was accessible to people. But I started with you, I've made you a character in a world that you're creating. A business gets built correctly, as you know, it should survive without either one of us, because it's sociologically built. You're instrumental to it now, but eventually Apple went on without Steve Jobs, but not before he built that world.

That's the thing. So I started with you, I've given you a, I don't want to say cartoonish, but I've certainly given you a dramatic flair, taking your personality as it exists and maybe accentuating a little bit, just like when I've taught this before, you take your personality and you just ratchet it up a few notches. Drama, people need dramatic examples to shake them out of their apathy, ie what the Batman Begins movie says, it's true. I'm starting at a very small scale with you, but look how you already have, you're bringing in Moshi now, he's becoming a character for example. He absolutely has a place, he's part of the roster, he's part of the cast of characters, he's in the world.

The same with your son, he's been helping out with some stuff, but believe me, he will have a much bigger presence, as you were talking about, and he will be part of this world. The people who joined just get their free test drive, they're part of that world if they want to be. They're going to have to engage a little bit and use the information and use the app and everything, but they're part of our world, but they're going to be able to go off and build their own world. It's interesting. It's really interesting and there's a lot of depth to this sort of thing, but we started, we are doing it. It doesn't just happen overnight, and I was even telling you, we were talking all about the group we're going to build within the app for our members.

I was going on and on, and on about this, remember the other day? Maybe I even lost you a little bit on some of that. But I think it will become very clear once you see it. It's going to be its own, it already is its own world, but it will become more and more, so as it fleshes out with more characters and more drama and just more natural storylines. I just call them storylines, but it's really just people interacting, businesses interacting with each other, going beyond just sharing value. I was telling you I might actually institute that rule, no sharing value. If it just becomes a place where people share tips, it becomes boring. You might as well be reading a textbook.

But if you make it its own world where people have to think a little bit differently, it expands the way they think and it challenges the way they think, and all of us, me too, all of us, it becomes something much, much greater than just a mere group. It becomes its own world. It's like I had to see the idea of a mobile app, I had to see it to really understand it, I think it's going to be the same with a lot of people who are watching this. Once you see it in action, and anyone watching this who was in my old elBenbo's Lair group knows exactly what I'm talking about, but it's hard to explain I think because it's just something you've got to see.

Anyone who's having trouble with this sort of thing and wants to understand it, once you build your own world, there's no buying from anyone else with your hardcore fans. Those people are only going to want to buy from you, regardless if you're the best option or whatever, there's always a better mousetrap, but there's not always a better world. You're going to have the best world, probably the only world that you're competing against. So I guess this turned into a sales pitch for a conference we haven't even started selling yet. That's the consequence of building a world. I'm going to say one more thing, Troy, because I think maybe this will help just as if you and I were talking and no one else was listening right now, which is how We've been doing this anyway. But just for your own, to help you understand it a little bit.

Do you remember when we did Wine Villains, right? It was something that I wanted to do and I got you and Misty roped in, it was our event, you and me, but she helped out a little bit with the babysitting everyone and all that. But she was very much a big part of elBenbo's Lair, I called her the Head Bitch in Charge, she had her own title and everything, so it was very much part of the world at the time. I'm pretty sure, now you tell me, how easy was it closing all those people? Because I was thinking about that, pretty much everyone in that room, as far as I can remember, maybe with one or two exceptions of 40 people, we had standing room only basically in that little wine room, it sold out in just a couple posts and a few emails. But the reality is a lot of those people were in my world and they wanted to meet the other people in the world in real life, and they weren't even necessarily there for the wine or to learn anything.

They were there to engage in the world that I had built that they loved being involved in, but in person and not just digitally through Facebook. But I'm guessing those were pretty easy sales for you to close, because they already wanted to buy, because they were already in that world and that's what it was. I'm not saying you didn't have to do any selling. But compared to probably if I had just sent that from an email list and they weren't in my world at that time, probably a lot harder. So this is not a small thing, I'm always thinking about it. The more you have someone in your world, the more likely they're going to buy, and not even want to buy from anyone else, quite frankly, because they want you. So I think that's it, but you tell me what you think.

TROY BROUSSARD: Yeah. No, I'm glad you went there with the last comment, because I think that allows us to bring us to a conclusion that will really speak to the people like myself that really look at what is the business proposition of this approach? I know that it's not just about business, but there are huge implications in business for this. You've already talked a lot about, from the Marvel to Apple and all the cultures that they built, well, look what it did for their business. So if you've been listening to Ben and I on our roadside rap here, as we're walking down and chatting across country back and forth and debating this and going deep, and if you've listened to it all and you're not really sure, well, I have to tell you, when you brought the Wine Villains stuff ...

The conversation was really funny because we started out with about, I think we started out with 20 people we were going to sell and then we went to 25 and then we ended up doing 35, and so it was funny when we had that first conversation and it was like, "Okay, we want to have 20 or 25 people there." Your first comment to me was, "Okay, so what? I need to get you 100 people to talk to?" I'm like, "Oh, hell no. Not only no, hell no do I want to have 100 phone calls." You get these people qualified as hell and afraid to talk to me that they better not waste my time, and let's do all this in email, so that by the time I get on the phone with them I'm just an order taker.

So, it was really fun, because it was the first time that you and I had that dynamic, and I ended up, and I told you, for 20 sales I probably needed 15 conversations, and you were like, "How in the hell are you going to get 20 sales out of 15 conversations?" Well, it's because on those, we had multiple people pay for multiple people to come. I knew that was going to be the case, and so we actually closed, that should be a whole training in and of itself at some day that we do, because we actually closed 130% of the sales. In other words, based on the number of sales calls, we had 135% that many sales.

It was a combination of a few things, it was a combination of the World-Building that you already had going on and people wanting to come and hang out with you, I'm not going to say anybody came to hang out with me, I think there was one or two people, but it was your list, it was your audience. So it wasn't about me, it was about them wanting to come and hang with Ben, was a big part of it. The other part of it was all of the preconditioning you had done in the emails to set up the call. Then the third part was just my style of sales. But it was funny, to give you an idea of how effective it was, I remember this one gentleman called and we had a call about it, and he was like, "Okay, well, we're in, I'm out on a walk. I'll get back to you later tomorrow and get this all wrapped up."

I'm like, "Dude, there is no tomorrow, there's today, there's this call. I'm not calling back a second time, this is a pretty impulse buy ticket purchase, so I'm not wasting my time making multiple calls. So, if you're in then that means I need a credit card right now." He says, "Well, I'm out on a walk and I'm out with the dogs, and I don't even have my wallet." I'm like, "Well, it's a phone, right? Put me on hold, call your wife, get a credit card and let's get this thing closed." It was so funny because that's exactly what he did. People will respond the way they're expected to respond. He knew that I wasn't joking around and he knew that you weren't joking around, because of the way it was set up that no, I'm not going to be chasing you for an order. You pay on the call or you don't and I go to the next person.

So, it was really funny, but here's this guy walking his dogs around town without even his wallet, and he's putting me on hold and texting his wife to get an order in and get it done right then on the call. So wrapping all this up, I just want to encourage you listening to this to realize that while Ben went deep down a rabbit hole of the psychology behind all of this and the history of it and giving you a lot of really good practical examples, at the end of the road it's about how do you grow your business and create a culture in your business that creates people, their desire to spend more with you, to be drawn in closer into the world that you've created? So hopefully, that brings it back to a bottom-line type summary, and Ben, I'll just let you add any final comments that you have before we wrap this up.

BEN SETTLE: I'll just end with this, if all this just seems a little murky still and you're having a hard time getting your mind wrapped around it, it's perfectly natural. I don't know very many people who think this way naturally. I do know people can be taught to think this way, but I got Stefania thinking this way. She absolutely never used to think this way and now she does, because she hears me talking about it and all that, so I know it can be taught. If this could be easily explained in one video, I would do it, but it's just not. This is years and years, and years thinking about it and doing it, experimenting with it, not even realizing it 90% of that time. So absorbing, being a student of this without even realizing.

At the time of this recording, we don't have an actual event plotted out or anything or know if or when we're going to do it. But I think that we should do it, get it done. If you're watching this and this is something you think you'd be interested in, let us know, one or both of us. I'd be very curious to see what people think about this topic and the idea of how it appeals to you and that sort of thing. Really, I can't think of a better way to create pre-sold customers than World-Building, so I'll just leave it at that.

New World Writer

Interviewed by David Garfinkel, World's Greatest Copywriting Coach
www.CopywritersPodcast.com

DAVID GARFINKEL: Let's get started with our guest, the notorious and endlessly fascinating Ben Settle. He's an email specialist, author, anti-professional and novelist. There are some rumors that he is planning to be the reincarnation of William Randolph Hearst. We'll talk about that later. People go nuts over Ben, including me. Once I wrote to him, "You're the effing hottest email copywriter on the web now." But I wasn't alone. Our recent guest, Richard Armstrong says, "I start my day with reading from the Holy Bible and Ben Settle's email, not necessarily in that order." And the normally sober Gary Bencivenga admits, "Good copy intoxicates me. Yours is high proof. I'm enjoying it."

Well, that pretty much gives you a picture of what other copywriters think about Ben. He's amazing. But Ben brings another skill to the party. Well, it is morbid. I have a morbid fascination with it and Ben has agreed to tell us about it today. He writes horror fiction. Let me read you this from the promo copy for one of his books. I was told, Ben, I may be mispronouncing a couple of words here so you can help me fix them later, maybe? *Zombie Cop*: The Enoch Wars, Book 1. And now the passage. If you're eating or drinking, you may want to listen to this part later.

> *"The blood was still warm and there was meat and what looked like veins between his teeth - hanging out like dental floss. Nobody knows where the still-living decapitated head came from. But when the head bites Police Chief Rawger, he becomes a zombie with an insatiable appetite for human flesh, revenge, and power. But, unlike Hollywood-depicted zombies, he can think, speak, and strategize. He's also deranged, sexually perverted, and takes absolute pleasure in his evil acts."*

Okay, I think you get the idea. So, what does this have to do with copy?

Nathan and I are hoping and praying we'll find out. And before we jump into the world of horror fiction, let's take a moment to remember some comforting words that help little children fall asleep safely at night. Copy is powerful. You're responsible for how you use what you hear on this podcast. And most of the time, common sense is all you need. But if you make extreme claims and/or if you're writing copy for offers and highly regulated industries like health, finance, and business opportunity, you may want to get a legal review after you write and before you start using your copy. My regular clients do this all the time.

Wow. Now let's get out our cloves of garlic for our personal protection and welcome Ben Settle. Ben, thank you so much for joining us today. I know you're moving, and it's logistically difficult and really appreciate you being here. Hi.

BEN SETTLE: Well, I got to say that was probably the coolest intro I've heard, and from a biased point of view, of course.

DAVID GARFINKEL: Well, I'll take it anyway. That's great. All right, well let's jump right in, huh? A lot of successful copywriters are interested in writing fiction, but most of us, including me, kind of balk when it comes to actually sitting down and writing a book. Not you. You got up on the mound and pitched. So tell us, how did this part of your interesting career all come about?

BEN SETTLE: Well, I used to be very intimidated by the idea of writing anything long, like a novel. And my novels are fairly short. I mean, I'm not writing War and Peace or anything like that. But yeah, sometime in 2010 I think, I was driving along and I had this idea of a zombie cop. What would happen if there was a zombified cop and he started pulling people over to eat them, kind of like a spider bringing flies into his trap, what would happen? And then I just started writing. I don't know. I think it helps, though, that I've been doing daily emails for so long that writing no longer intimidates me. I treated every chapter basically like an email. So, I wrote... most of these books are 14 chapters. And I just would write one chapter a day and I'd be done with the first draft.

DAVID GARFINKEL: And how long is a chapter? As long as short email?

BEN SETTLE: Yeah, I mean they're not that short, but 10 pages on average. I don't know. They seem to have gotten shorter with every book. *Zombie Cop* was the longest, and by the time I got to the seventh book, I mean it was basically a novella at that point. I don't know if that was because I ran out stuff to say, or I just had tighter writing. I don't know. But it worked out for me.

DAVID GARFINKEL: Well, you know what? I mean, if you look at James

Patterson's stuff, and he's sort of like the industral author. I mean literally he has a system and he has other people do it and stuff. His chapters are sometimes one or two pages in the book itself, so that just may be the way things are going and you're just part of the train, right?

BEN SETTLE: Yeah, and just from a commercial point of view, and I haven't really heavily marketed these books at all, but you'll make a lot more money as a novelist writing shorter books than you will longer ones because you can get more books out and selling. The more you write, the more you make. That's the whole thing about writing. I've learned this, and this is good for all of us who were not born with writing talent, which I certainly wasn't. The whole key is the more words you write, the more money you make in any kind of writing profession. So, if you write more words than you do now, faster than you do now, you'll make more money, including fiction.

DAVID GARFINKEL: That's actually a good point that a lot of people overlook. I'm really glad you brought it up. I mean, sounds simple but profound and a lot of people who are just waiting for the perfect inspiration or scared or something, they're only cheating themselves. So let's talk a little more about the book. When you have an idea for a book, what are the steps you go through from driving down the road and thinking, "Oh God, I hope the next cop who stops me isn't a zombie and eats me rather than giving me a ticket" to actually getting the book written. What do you go through?

BEN SETTLE: Well, I had the idea for several years before I started actually writing it, probably like 3 years. And I have a friend, his name's Robert Bruce. I don't know if you guys know him or not. And I got to talking to him and I said, "You know, I have this idea." And he goes, "Ben, just write it." I go, "Yeah, but I really suck at dialogue." And he goes, "Ah, don't worry about it. You just write as fast as you can and then go back and you can fix stuff later." And I realized it's not unlike writing sales copy. You just get it down and then you can go back and it's like movies, which are actually really made in the editing room. It's very similar.

DAVID GARFINKEL: Do you enjoy this enough so you'll want to do other stuff?

BEN SETTLE: Well, I do want to do other stuff, but I have this bug to take a shot at turning *Zombie Cop* into a screenplay and just seeing what happens.

DAVID GARFINKEL: Wow.

BEN SETTLE: I would love to do that.

DAVID GARFINKEL: We talk a lot on this podcast about taking techniques from writing fiction to writing copy. And we have had another novelist on here, in fact Richard Armstrong, one of your big fans, just a few weeks ago, but We've never had anyone who writes material as intense as you do. I'm talking about your fiction, although I could be talking about your emails. We've never had anyone like that on here before. Could you share what's different and what's similar about writing fiction and writing email?

BEN SETTLE: Think of writing as the human body and fiction is working your legs and writing nonfiction is working your upper body. It's two different total muscles. You know what I mean? Writing fiction is just completely different, more exhausting, but it's all writing. You have to tap more into a narrative with fiction. I think copywriters will all make the best novelists, simply because if we're doing it right, we're trained to really work on that attention span and we get bored probably easily. If we're paranoid about boring our readers, we're not going to bore people like a lot of novels do because we're so paranoid. I know I am when I'm writing copy and I'm sure you are too. "Am I boring them at this sentence?"

A lot of fiction is boring. But if you go in there with this kind of copywriter mindset, maybe that's why the books are so short. I don't know. I'm just paranoid. I'm writing this stuff and I think copywriters just have a huge advantage if they use that because it's all about not boring people, keeping their attention, roping them in, telling stories, creating images. All the stuff we do writing copy except we're writing complete fiction. Well, hopefully most copywriters are not writing complete fiction in their ads, but some of them do.

DAVID GARFINKEL: There's a lot of dangers to that. One thing I'm particularly interested in, and we talked about this on the podcast a while ago but I think you have a much better perspective than anyone else I can think of, is the whole issue of you want to have a narrative going on in your fiction. That's what the legs do. They walk somewhere. Copywriters want to put the person's credit card in your little device with your arms. What's the danger? And Nathan said something brilliant about this in the previous podcast, that sometimes when a story in copy is too good, you're going to get people so emotionally worked up with the story that you're going to lose them for the rest of the copy. Could you talk at all about the limits of narrative in copy and maybe even things you had to work on or things you see other people doing that they should stop doing?

BEN SETTLE: I've been thinking about this a lot lately and it's kind of ironic we're talking about this. Probably around 2008, 2009, I wrote a whole bunch of sales letters for this guy named Captain Chris Pizzo. He used to be the number one guy selling—

DAVID GARFINKEL: The big fighting guy. Yeah, I know him.

BEN SETTLE: Yeah, yeah. Now he does other stuff, but he was number one at the time. And what I loved about working with him is he didn't just create products and sell them. This guy created a world. He was a world builder and we very consciously, every product was a different story, usually about him or someone he knew. Every product was based on a different Special Forces guy. One was a Green Beret. The other guy was, what are they in the British? SAS? One guy was a Navy Seal. But it was like you weren't just buying stuff from him. You were in his world. He created a world. He even was telling me, "Ben, we should write screenplays based on this." And I think it would probably do well because he did such a good job of building a world.

If you built this world around your products, around your personality and all of that, I find that a lot of problems disappear when it comes to people believing you, when it comes to people's skepticism and all that. There's nothing new about what I'm about to say. I mean, Earl Nightingale was saying it more than 70 years ago, but they're not really buying the product. They're buying us. They're really buying you. They're not really buying what you're selling. They're buying you. It makes sense to put you as much as you can, or your client if you're working for clients, as much personality into that as possible. I've never had that problem where I've told a story so well that they didn't buy it. But I think this idea of World-Building is just something that's lost on a lot of people.

DAVID GARFINKEL: I want to take a moment to point out how vitally important headlines are in copy. As you may already know, the strength of your headline accounts for up to 80 or even 90% of the effectiveness of your ad. Think about that. What if there were a way to shortcut the headline writing process and start a new headline based on a proven winner? Well, there is. It's all in my book called *Advertising Headlines That Make You Rich*. This book is available now on amazon.com. *Advertising Headlines That Make You Rich*. What's unique about this book is it shows you exactly how to adapt a proven winner to your product or service, because I show you 10 adaptations for each headline in different niches and explain the psychology of how to adapt a headline. *Advertising Headlines That Make You Rich* in hard copy and Kindle formats on Amazon. Now, back to our show.

That's a great point. In terms of putting you into the copy, it's very interesting because I've had a couple of conversations with people about that in the last week, and my contention and my experience, based on doing a lot of critique, is that the creative copywriter artiste types, and I'm not saying that in a sneering way. I'm just saying the more creative type people, if anything, they might put too much of themselves into the story or put too much of themselves into their copy. But business owners, business types, who've been taught to edit themselves out of everything and just focus on the product or the features or the benefits or whatever, don't put their personality in enough.

I think the way you're talking about building an attractive world around yourself or even an individual product and inviting the prospect in so that they can partake in the benefits, the joys, the pleasures, the drama, whatever. That's a cool thing. What do you think about that?

BEN SETTLE: You know, you just reminded me of something that the three of us can probably all remember. I say three of us, you, me and Nathan, but probably certain listeners of your show, we can all remember that crazy ridiculous Facebook group I used to have, elBenbo's Lair.

DAVID GARFINKEL: Oh yeah, I remember.

BEN SETTLE: Yeah. Okay. So, I will tell you, I've only talked about this in my newsletter before, but that whole thing was an experiment in World-Building. That's all it was ever intended to be, and it took a life of its own. I was able to sell stuff without even having to really sell stuff because this world was created. It was only supposed to be entertainment and satire but I literally had people in there thinking that I wanted to impregnate certain girls in there. The weirdest thing. It was so weird.

When I ended it, it was such a relief because this thing had taken a life of its own, like one of my monsters in my books. But that's World-Building, right? It took this life of its own world where people wanted to be a part of it. I was not even letting everybody in. I was purposely shutting people out. And I mean, it was this weird thing and I just kept thinking, "Okay, what else can I do to build another block of this world?" And I would throw, "Oh, okay, I'm going to have an immigration policy. This is a wall."

DAVID GARFINKEL: And oh man, I'm so glad you said that. I never quite understood what you were doing with that and that puts it into perspective. And yeah, in terms of business, it worked. It's way different than trying to be Saturday Night Live in your emails or something, right? I mean, this is the most serious and both I think the highest and the lowest use of fiction and drama really. I do want to talk about emails a little, if we could pivot to that. Okay?

BEN SETTLE: Okay.

DAVID GARFINKEL: So, your emails are consistently bolder and more provocative than almost any others I've seen. And maybe I just haven't seen enough to see the ones that are even bolder and more provocative than yours. I'm just wondering, would you say that you have rewritten the rules for yourself, or did you just decide a long time ago that there are no rules?

BEN SETTLE: Yeah, it all started, the whole mindset behind this started probably back in like 2003 before I knew anything about email at all. I don't know how you would find this now unless you know people who run the, they're not GKIC anymore. I guess they're No BS Inner Circle, whatever it is now. They keep changing the name. But if you know the guys who run that, you could probably find this because the new president asked me about this. He said, "Hey, you mentioned this interview. I'm going through the archives. Where is it?"

Well, it was an interview Dan Kennedy did with this guy named Peter Montoya. Peter Montoya is a personal branding guy and I think he writes to a more traditional business audience. He said something that I never forget and I'm always thinking about, even to this day, and that is, he goes, "You won't know you've gone too far until you've gone too far at least one time." I have yet to go too far, David. I keep trying, but it doesn't seem to happen.

DAVID GARFINKEL: I get that. Your whole mission is push the envelope to see where it breaks or to see where I'm a violator or something like that? Is that right? And so far in all your explorations, you haven't found that place?

BEN SETTLE: Yeah, and it's not like a matter of "oh, I'm going to be offensive or anything." It's just being as personality driven as I can and I don't even really get that personal with people. I just don't have any governor. Have you ever rented a U-Haul truck or something? They put a governor on it so you can't go past 50 miles per hour, or whatever they set it at. I just don't have a governor. Whatever's on my mind, I say it and it doesn't seem to really have a limit yet.

DAVID GARFINKEL: Yeah, I don't find you offensive. I find you provocative. I think there's a big difference. But anyway, it's a distinction we could spend half an hour on and only you and I and Nathan would care. Could you give us a few ... For people who still have governors or don't even understand that concept of physics, could you give us a few Ben Settle tips for writing emails that get noticed and get responses? Anything?

BEN SETTLE: Yeah, well the first thing to do is for people listening to this, I mean I know that copywriters were taught to have swipe files and all that. I don't believe in really having those anymore. I think you should when you're starting out to learn and all that and I still study ads, but you almost want to do the opposite. It's all about violating your industry's norms, which is another thing I learned from Dan Kennedy. What is everybody doing? Well in email, I see everybody doing certain things. They're making their emails look pretty and all that. So I've always been a plain text guy. That's easy to violate. I see people only sending an email when they have something to say, which isn't necessarily bad, but there's a subconscious thing going on with your readers. Well, you're supposed to be this expert at what you do. You don't have something to say every day? That was something the great Matt Furey once said, that I have never forgotten. They're not thinking that consciously, but if they're getting emails from your competitors every day and not you. So, I'm trying to send more emails. In fact, one email a day isn't enough for me now. Now I'm starting to send two or three a day. And it's little things like that. Just think of all the things you're not supposed to do and then just do the opposite and see what happens. This is also a function of World-Building too, incidentally. Really, everything you do or even everything you don't do is.

DAVID GARFINKEL: I love it. I love it. I can sort of... Nathan, you might want to jump in here. I remember Halbert saying he was a giant meat cleaver that would cut through the audience and pulverize them. I think what Ben just said, our audience is going to be like that. Half of them are going, "Yeah, you go boy," and the other half are going, "Oh no. Mommy, did you hear what Ben said?" So that's really, I love that. So, tell us about Email Players and then I have one more ... people want to get it. What is it? Can they still get it and what do they do?

BEN SETTLE: Well Email Players is a monthly print newsletter. It's email, but I veer off the reservation sometimes and talk about other related stuff about copywriting, persuasion, all that. The best way to check that out is just to get the free issue I give away at BenSettle.com when you opt in and then you can see if you like it or not. But that's a free issue so you can test it. You can see if I'm full of crap or not. Whatever you want to do with it.

DAVID GARFINKEL: BenSettle.com. And then if you don't mind, unless it's under wraps or you have some NDA with a BC or a PE or a whatever, can you talk about this publishing empire that you're building?

BEN SETTLE: Well, I've been learning a lot from Dan Kennedy my whole business career, but mostly lately I've really been honing in on certain things I've heard him say almost off the cuff. He made me realize once when I was listening to this thing he was doing. What business are you really in? I mean, I'm not really a copywriter. I realize I'm becoming more of a publisher. I publish a print newsletter. I publish emails every day. I publish novels and business-related books. I have this medium. I think everyone should try to control their own media eventually because that way you're not at the wiles of being de-platformed and all this. I realized I want to focus more on that—the publishing side and me being a publisher.

Now that has a lot more potential to it than just an email specialist. I've been rapidly creating products and turning my old audio and video products into print books, which is another violation of industry norms. I have no digital component to these products and they're more expensive than when they were digital. And I'm going to put together a way where people can sell those, but not through a traditional affiliate channel. It'll be something completely different. But that's a whole other aspect. If it works, it's going to grow things quite rapidly. If it doesn't, then so what? But I'm thinking more like a publisher now and less as just an email guy. Again, it's all World-Building.

DAVID GARFINKEL: Okay. Wow. Well, this is fascinating. I enjoy that when we have a chance to get together, which is rare. I've always enjoyed that. And yeah, Ben, thank you for being on.

SPEAKER 1: Make sure to subscribe, rate, and review on iTunes so you'd never miss an episode. This show was brought to you by the Copy and Funnels podcast network.

Appendix One
–
Laying Down Your Lair

This is a passage from my book *Social Lair*—which is about how I created one of the single most engaged Facebook groups in my niche, and monetized it. It also talks about World-Building from a social media perspective. To be notified next time it is on sale, make sure you're on my daily email list at:

www.BenSettle.com

Following is the Framework and "ground floor" foundations that made elBenbo's Lair tick. When I first started it, it was your basic, ordinary, run-of-the-mill, & completely plain vanilla boring group like everyone else's. In other words, I gave *Value!* and I made sure to "interact with people" and I would "keep engaging with members" and then let it go in whatever direction it wanted. Which usually meant it didn't go anywhere. Then one night I was sitting in a bar waiting for a chick I was meeting up with. I was drinking one of the 3 or 4 beers available on tap at that particular bar. So, for shyts and giggles, I went into elBenbo's Lair and created a mindless contest.

The contest:

Whoever could guess what beer I was drinking would get some kind of prize.

The result:

The First elBenbo's Lair Thread-Hole.

I'll talk more about Thread-Holes later.

For now, just realize that one question, and the intense interest people had in this boring subject started a chain of events that turned into something akin to a giant time *and* attention-sucking creature created in a secret government lab. Specifically, when my friend Tim private messaged me just a few minutes after the post where I'd already had over two dozen comments — when most *Value!* posts revealing information people would have to pay a lot of money to learn would not get half that many total:

"25 comments on what kind of beer Ben is drinking.... they're wrapped around your finger but good"

That was the moment of clarity.

I had watched for weeks prior how my group would react to certain off-the-wall posts, ideas, contests, and thoughts I put in there. But I wasn't sufficiently bored enough to exploit such knowledge or sufficiently aware enough to realize the power having such knowledge contained. So I immediately started concocting a plan in that bar for doing what can only be described as a...

Mad Social Experiment.

I was going to flip the board.

Scatter the pieces all over the place.

And turn this asset I did not realize I had until that moment — an already engaged audience, due to years of daily emails where I had already bonded with them, built a relationship with them, and created a customer list with them — into something...

Completely off the Charts Different.

However, before I continue the story, a tangent.

It's a big tangent, though, so read it carefully. Without this tangent nothing else in this book will have nearly as much context. Nothing you learn will be nearly as profitable. And nothing you do with it will have nearly as much impact on your business. With that in mind, notice I said "already engaged" audience. Specifically, from years of doing aggressive email marketing. Nothing else you see in this book will work as well — except maybe in very unique circumstances, with very unique personalities, with already-established audiences on certain other platforms — without understanding this secret sauce that made this whole concoction edible and pleasing and not poisonous and bitter:

An Engaged Email List I Already Had a Strong and *Established* Relationship with.

This was a list I'd already been mailing daily.

With people who already knew, liked, & trusted me.

And that was already, in many cases, populated not just with leads & opt-ins, but buyers and *Email Players* subscribers. I'm not saying you *"must have!"* an already-engaged email list to make what you learn in this book work on at least a small scale. I am simply saying that is what made it work for me. In my case, I did not build elBenbo's Lair from within Facebook or recruit members from any other social media platform. I built it from my list of daily email readers, *Email Players* subscribers, and other buyers…

Exclusively.

This is no exaggeration:

I cannot think of a single time where I so much as even passively mentioned elBenbo's Lair's existence to my main Facebook timeline, Twitter audience, or LinkedIn connections (the only social media I was on). I didn't want random people in there. That said, I admittedly can see how the Social Lair methodology in this book could work with someone who has a big enough amd engaged enough existing social media audience, or an audience already gathered together in a "herd" in some other media. Like, for example, if you have a hyper-engaged YouTube audience who loves watching your videos. Or a gigantic Facebook following that already hangs on every post you make. Or a big blog readership that rabidly comments and engages with you there. I just have never seen anyone do it to the extent elBenbo's Lair did, because I've never seen anyone do what I did precisely the way I did it.

So, whether it's email or any other media…

Without Having an Existing Relationship None of this Works.

They have to come in *already* knowing you.

You should also already know many of them.

And then, as you execute the Social Lair methodology, from there it should be mostly just word-of-mouth. In the case of elBenbo's Lair, people came because other members couldn't stop talking about it. Sometimes it was because I'd horrified someone. Many times, it was because of a 500+ comment Thread-Hole that took a bizarre turn and people wanted their friends to see it. But most of the time it was because it'd gained an almost cult-like popularity of its own, where…

It Was a Privilege and Not a Right to be up in elBenbo's Lair.

It was like an exclusive club.

The kind you had to know someone to get inside I never begged, pleaded with, or asked people to join. I simply let them have the opportunity to come to its gates at certain times I deemed fit. My Immigration Policy sifted and sorted them there. After that, the member's willingness to follow the rules and laws determined if they stayed. And over time, their ability to think for themselves and contribute to Thread-Holes, their ability to resist the urge to Virtue-Signal and Self-Victimize, and their ability to be relevant without trying to give Value or say something stupid out of a needy desire to be heard… kept them inside as productive members of the Society, with everyone else either ejected, leaving on their own, or simply observing & learning and being entertained by it all. But no matter who they were, or where they came from…

It All Started with Email.

Not with social media.

I populated my Society from the very beginning to the very end only with my email list, and never from within my existing social media audiences. There's nothing new, of course, about sending an email list to a social media platform to begin to build an audience there. But, the way I did it, the foundational Laws put in place you'll be reading about next, combined with the antics I'll be telling you about in the next section that kept people coming back… along with the ways I "laced" the group together into a strong family-type unit of berserkers and lurkers — where even those who disagreed with each other all the time became life-long friends, JV partners, and even marriage partners…

Made It a 100% Unique Entity unto Itself.

And if I hadn't started with a foundation of my email list — that I'd spent the prior 14+ years building a relationship with already — I don't think it would have worked out the way it did. In fact, the very nature of how I created it caused another phenomenon to happen.

A phenomenon I call:

"Email List Laundering"

Yes, I *laundered* my list.

Not unlike a drug dealer, in some ways.

It isn't the exact same, of course. But like a drug dealer cleans their money both literally in a washing machine and also figuratively by circulating it as fast as possible into other holdings — I laundered my email list, turning what was already a responsive and engaged email list into a list I believe is now…

Easily the Single Most Responsive and
Engaged List in My Niche to this Day.

At least going by what my JV partners report.

Take, for example, Brian Kurtz. I've had the privilege to know and talk to Brian many times, and have spoken at some of his infamous Master Classes.

He cut his teeth during the 1980's in direct marketing and helped build a 9 million name database from which he oversaw 1.5 billion pieces of mail while curating, testing, and mailing thousands of mailing lists. And this was in the direct mail days, where it was much harder and cost a lot more than it does online, obviously. Anyway, here's what he said about my email list:

> **"While so many people adhere to the premise that 'size matters,' when it comes to great lists, audiences and tribes, I will take smaller and mightier lists over large lists anytime. And a perfect example of this is Ben Settle's list…which calling it simply a 'list' does it a disservice. Ben promoted my 'Titans of Direct Response' package…a somewhat esoteric but powerful product which included videos, interviews and swipe files for the ages…but it needed lots of support and explanation to sell well. And he outsold every other affiliate I used for this program, almost all of which had larger lists than his…but clearly not as responsive. He even outsold others with lists 10 times the size of his."**

That's just one of many examples. And while my list is responsive for a lot of reasons, I have traced a huge bulk of its responsiveness to…

How I Ran My Email List through elBenbo's Lair.

It's obvious when I look at my most rabid readers, buyers, and those who reply to my daily musings, and see how many were "laundered" through elBenbo's Lair.

Here is how it works:

- You send your main email list to your elBenbo's Lair-style social media platform.

- From there you run Social Lair game (what the rest of this book is about) on those followers.

- And then from your elBenbo's Lair-style social media platform you periodically — organically, whenever it makes sense — send those members directly (via links, product purchases, etc.) back out into your *other* media platforms, where they are far more engaged with every word you write or say, far more excited about being in your World, and far more…

Eager to Buy Everything You Sell.

The quality of buyer can be almost unbelievable.

As can be the quality of the *relationship* you have with those buyers. Especially because after you launder them like this — assuming your offers genuinely improve their lives, of course — they can become almost hyper-loyal to you, grateful to you almost to a fault, and surprisingly eager to do business with you in whatever other ways they can.

Here is what Email List Laundering looks like:

Email list

elBenbo's Lair-style

Social media platform/forum/message board

All other platforms you use to market and sell with — including, but not at all limited to:

- Podcast
- Mobile app
- Website
- Public speaking/events you teach at
- Masterminds
- Direct mail list
- Product sales
- Premiums and swag (these are platforms unto themselves if used correctly)
- Anywhere else you teach, sell, or have content

Since they are still on your email list this whole time, then by doing the above, you've now laundered them. And if you did it right, you should also have made them…

Far More Responsive when You Sell to Them via Email Henceforth.

Thus goes Email List Laundering.

Obviously, I can't promise you'll get the exact same results. But I can say that I have watched people I've given advice to on these matters do only some of what you're reading in this book (and often completely half-assed)… and see much better results from their social media and other marketing endeavors than they had been getting. Which is why I believe it can be just an extremely powerful phenomenon if you do it right. And while I left Facebook never to return — and do not recommend it for a whole host of reasons I'll touch on later — the key is finding a social media platform (even a forum or message board will do… it does not have to be anything big tech, and I'd argue it shouldn't be due to lack of control) where you can "isolate" people into your own corner of it.

That way it can be used with direct marketing 101:

"Build a List and Mail It"

In this case, it's two lists:

Your email list, and also another "list" which is that social media platform where you can isolate them from the rest of the world, and communicate with them privately, without the outside world (we'll just call 'em *normies*) knowing about it, much less being in there clogging everything up with the usual social media timeline nonsense of food pics, Virtue Signaling, giving Value, and the list goes on. I will cover all this in far more depth. Worry not if any of this isn't 100% clear yet.

All right, necessary tangent over.

Back to That Fateful Night at the Bar:

I realized my entire business — especially elBenbo's Lair — could be far more than a mere group or place to socialize or a platform to sell on. It was a potentially big part of my business's World. i.e., it was another aspect of my ongoing business World-Building campaign. World-Building is something I'd been consciously doing with my business for over two years prior, and unconsciously doing for 10+ years before that automatically, due to my childhood summers full of playing RPGs, writing fiction, and thinking up new World's in my head, anyway.

Onward with the story:

For whatever dumb reason, I just hadn't thought of using my Facebook group in my World-Building antics. I think mostly because I never was much a fan of Facebook — or social media in general — in the first place. I always knew it had its place, though. And so, I was on it to that extent, including having my own group, obviously. Plus, I'd run another group prior to elBenbo's Lair with my pal Ryan Healy called Street-Smart Biz. The original inspiration for having these groups was due to something Russell Brunson said during one of the Oceans 4 Masterminds I hosted with some of my pals at the time. Oceans 4 were "hot seat" masterminds. And Russell was a client at one of them. During his hot seat he told us about how he used his own Facebook group to encourage people to *brag* about how they use his products to become successful in order to turn the group into a sort of testimonial-generation machine. I thought that was an extremely smart idea. And, thus, I created my own group with Ryan, and then later elBenbo's Lair on my own.

Long Story Short:

I saw that, yes, my group produced testimonials.

And to that end it served its purpose. But that night at the bar I realized it had more potential than just being a way to make money or get testimonials or to sell in. In my way of thinking, it was not only a solid part of my World, it was also…

Its Own Society *within* My World.

Worlds are made up of societies and people.

At least, the inhabited kinds are.

And as I write about in *elBenbo Press*, I consider my books and newsletter and other offers to each be their own characters and citizens in my World. But my email list, to me, was always a Society of people *within* my World where they interacted with my offers.

That may sound a bit weird.

But that is simply how I look at my business.

And the way I see it:

Everything a Business Does is World-Building.

Yes, whether you realize it or not.

World-Building is everything a business does and everything it doesn't do, and is embedded in everything that business experiences. It's an intangible concept based on someone's unique peculiarities, skills, preferences, and assets, not anyone else's. It's also a big concept, that has many moving parts and details that can't be reduced to a checklist. But like it or not, believe it or not, care about it or not… every business engages in World-Building. You may or may not do a particularly good job at it. And, in my experience and observation, 99.9% of marketers and businesses have no idea they are doing it at all, much less correctly. And, because of that, they do it in a completely random and reactionary way. Thus, their World-Building "game" sucks at best, and is…

Counterproductive at Worst.

In the case of elBenbo's Lair:

I knew I had another Society-in-the-shaping within the World I'd been building for nearly 15 years by the time I founded the group. This Society was mostly already there: the people, the houses, the buildings, even the crude underpinnings of a *government*. I just had to flesh it out, plot out how I wanted it to look, and build a foundation for the aggressive and hair-raising ideas I wanted to implement after doing so, where those antics would do the most good and have the most impact. It was now beyond just a way to make money, or get testimonials, or engage with my customers and leads. Those things, I figured (and it turned out I was correct), would take care of themselves if I but built-out this Society, and ran it the way I will show you throughout the rest of this book.

Thus, back to the first big and most important change:

It was not a "group" it was a...

Bustling Society unto Itself.

And that was what all the idiot copycats trying to duplicate the success of elBenbo's Lair never understood or grasped. They were simply too stupid to figure it out, too shallow thinking to think beyond "copy and paste!", and/or too lazy to plot-out and arrange all the various elements, variables, and moving parts necessary to create a true Society on a social media platform. While all the other groups in my niche and market were run by Gary Vee worshippers chanting "Give Value!" and populated with people trying to grandstand to show how smart they were, while trying to poach clients & customers on the sneak (and often not even on the sneak)... and while those group owners allowed such activity because that's just how it was "supposed" to be done, I decided to do...

The Complete Opposite.

And I did it in every way I could think of.

It's interesting to think back about how, at that time, I hadn't yet heard the great Dan Kennedy's magnificent teaching about defying the norms of your industry. In the teaching I heard, he advised making a big, fat list of all the norms of your industry: What everyone does just because that's what everyone does. And then, go through that list, one-by-one, and literally *defy* them by doing the opposite. According to him — and this has certainly been the case whenever I've done it — *your business grows in exact proportion to how many norms you defy, and how ruthlessly you do it*. It may very well be the single easiest way to make more sales, build a more influential & popular brand, and create customers that want to buy your every offer — if for no other reason than you are completely different from everything else they see. What's different stands out, after all. And what stands out gets the lion's share of attention. And while I can't speak for anyone else's results in such cases, in elBenbo's Lair's case I didn't just defy the norms...

I Defiled and Profaned Them.

And I did both as ruthlessly as possible.

In my experience, defiling what the so-called social media gurus do is like a devious and underhanded way to get them to build your influence, audience, and business. And that's why I suggest, in whatever way you decide to use this book on social media, you do the same. Defile and profane the norms of what everyone else is doing — including anything you see in *this* book that may now be a "norm" today or in the future. I haven't been on social media for a long time. Yet, I have heard some brave souls have tried implementing some of my nutty antics from elBenbo's Lair.

But it all starts with building a Society, first.

Appendix Two
–
Don't Build a Business, Build a World

This passage is from my book elBenbo Press, which is about my high-ticket book and newsletter publishing model. The entire methodology heavily uses several World-Building concepts, including many you have not read about in this book. To be notified next time this book is on sale, make sure you're on my daily email list:

www.BenSettle.com

This is what separates the men from the boys. It's what will also separate you from anyone else you compete against. In fact, I daresay you will not even have any rea; "competition" once you start doing business by this rule.

What do I mean by "build a World?"

To explain this, I have no choice but to tell you a story about when the CEO of a New York firm that helps authors create a book and then connects them with sought-after editors in the industry sent me some feedback.

Specifically, she said two things:

1. She's *not* the biggest fan of my emails

1. But, she said she read my *Zombie Cop* novel (the first book in the seven book *Enoch Wars* series), said it was good, and that the book had a great sense of pacing and *World-Building*. Then she graciously offered to connect me with an agent (not what her company does, so nothing in it for her)

Anyway, Here's what's important about this:

She got me thinking about something hardly any other marketers think about. And that is, the idea of World-Building. I had been doing it for years in my business, without really thinking about it. And the reason why is, to me it's very natural after mindlessly spending my youth in cahoots with my friends playing *Dungeons & Dragons* and other RPG 's. Building worlds, characters, adventures, narratives, story arcs, and that sort of thing comes very easily due to that. And it was just as easy to bring that to my marketing, to my brand, and to my business as a whole.

For example:

I once ran an insanely addictive — according to many of its members, at least — Facebook group called *elBenbo's Lair*. I built a "World" full of surprises, rules, laws, languages, customs, characters, storylines, plot twists, and other such hijinx that made it so it wasn't unusual to have someone call it "real life" with everything outside the group being ignored. Sometimes there were so many Thread-holes and discussions, debates, and arguments going on concurrently that people would post stuff on their main timeline they'd rather not the public see, thinking they were safely in my group…

Only to Have Their Friends and Family Think They Were Nuts.

Such was the power of building my own World.

Very few people (if any) in marketing understand how to world-build like this. And even many of those who do, appear to do it on accident. Some examples of business people that World-Build include the late Walt Disney and the late Steve Jobs. Nintendo has at times done this quite brilliantly, too. In the direct marketing industry one of the only people I see doing this is the great Dan Kennedy. His whole "Planet Dan" world is quite brilliant. To make an apt analogy inspired by a truly great World-Builder (C.S. Lewis), in my own case I look at my own business as a sort of Narnia.

In other words:

You find your way into my World through any number of "doorways" peppered throughout the internet and also offline. (Referrals, word-of-mouth, physical books I sell, when mentioned on stage from people speaking, being plugged as a useful resource on coaching calls, when I am interviewed on podcasts, via one of my "list swinging" campaigns, etc.). For the sake of this analogy, let's say you found the wardrobe doorway into my World. You come inside and it looks a lot different than anywhere else you've seen in my niche. From the way I write and sell with emails, the kinds of offers I promote, the way my books look and feel, the personality I project, the expectations I have of my customers, and a hundred other little peculiarities that set my business and my brand apart from everything else you've seen. My goal is for it to be almost sort of "magical" in the sense that it's not like anything else out there. Especially compared to the myriad number of loser copycats who try to ape everything I do…

Only to Look Like a Fax of a Xerox Copy of a Scan of a Piece of Reproduced Art Created by Someone Else.

That's the contrast I go for.

But now you're inside my World reading my emails, clicking to my sites, checking out my free mobile apps, consuming my content, and wandering around. It's a bit *nippy* in my World, though. My World also has its own strangely unique laws, customs, rules, and even its own language, too. I have multiple storylines about my life and/or different ways of doing things running through my daily emails. I give people options for thinking differently, rather than just confirming their existing biases to challenge their assumptions and shake them out of their goo-roo casino ways. I'm very blunt and don't mince words or try to hide what I think of certain types of people. I gleefully mock laziness, bad ideas, and dangerous teachings floating around my industry. I call out bull shyt when I see it — including *my* own bull shyt, at times, as I'm certainly not perfect, and am even noticeably flawed. And I am quick to eject trolls (and also gratefully use their comments to make sales with via email), complainers, and those who need hand-holding for the slightest of offenses. Plus, I immediately block people who subscribe and then cancel my paid newsletter, and basically freeze them out by never communicating with them again, or easily letting them buy my *other* offers in the cases where I can control that process.

So yes, it's a bit wintery in elBenbo's Lair — in his "World."

So, you best grab one of those coats from the wardrobe.

And when you venture further inside my World, you start seeing even more things that set me and my business and my brand apart from everyone else's. Especially the ones that all mimic and copy each other, as well as copying the same people teaching the same nonsense, to the same "gene pool" of leads, who do business in a very drab and boring fashion like everyone else. What you see next is going to depend on you and your preferences and what your curiosity wants to look more closely at. Again, it's not unlike the Narnian experience. You see odd things that don't "belong" and thus instantly stick out. You see the equivalent of a burning lamp post in the middle of the forest. You see a faun nervously running around in the snow carrying parcels. The animals are talking and trying to keep you away from a witch chasing them, with Father Christmas right behind. You can choose which part you want to explore. Do you have tea with the faun? Go to the White Witch 's castle? Eat fish and have a conversation with the talking Beavers? Whatever the case, you know there's a lot more to this World than what you are used to.

You see offers for products and services that seem different, too. They aren't

Ben Settle

being pitched at you by desperate, needy marketers.

If anything…

The Offers Are Saying You Probably Should *Not* Buy, Along with Legitimate Reasons Why.

In other words, you are never "sold."

You are merely given the opportunity to buy.

And you are given this opportunity not via fancy whiz-bang technology, Facebook and mobile text bots, or prettied-up graphics riddled with advanced tracking links. It happens almost exclusively via plain text emails with a strong pitch to buy something — and never by a series of weak "nurturing" emails sent by amateurs who have no clue how to sell, and think just giving away freebies is the way to some kind of prosperity. These emails in my World give you the opportunity to keep traveling to castle Cair Paravel on the eastern shores with a throne made just for you, that will teach you (due to the nature of what I sell) how to rule your own kingdom and have your own World. Sometimes you will even see Father Christmas popping up with a sale for my offers, at steep discounts — gifts for you, that you did not expect, and are hard to refuse. And this goes on for however long it takes you to travel through my World and buy one of my offers where you ultimately get to see me — the "Aslan" of my World — waiting for you, guiding you, and wanting to help you.

But Only If You Faithfully Do the Work and Make it There on Your Own Accord.

Yes, my friend, there is no hand-holding or "nurturing."

And when you reach your destination, when you are crowned a king or queen of your own domain, I may leave you be for a while, as I have other Worlds/Businesses — mobile app companies, novels/comic book line, etc.— to attend. But I will always be back with more adventures to send you on.

Again, there are many doorways into my World.

Frankly, there are more doorways than I can keep track of anymore built up from 20 years in the business, making connections, building a network, circulating content, selling offers, and sending daily emails in the way I teach in my *Email Players* newsletter. I don't worry so much about which doorway someone finds me with. And there are many doorways I deliberately have not built (paid traffic), too, that I could build should I choose to.

Plus, not everyone stays in my World.

Some do, many don't. In fact, most don't. Like Susan in the Narnia books, she loved it when she was there, was told she couldn't come back when she was sent back home, and bitterly lost all memory of the place, even mocking it later to her siblings and friends who still loved the place and yearned to return. So, it is with people I blacklist or those who simply don't resonate with my World, my way of doing things, and my philosophies and methods.

My World is a small World.

A World meant for a very specific kind of customer.

A World that, quite frankly…

Is *Rife* with Obstacles and Reasons to Leave!

And like Aslan, elBenbo is not a "tame" lion.

I don't react to my list's every demand.

And I don't believe the customer is always right, either. If anything, it's the opposite. And instead of being polite and nice and blowing sunshine up your bum to hopefully get you to like me… to hopefully get you to buy from me… and to hopefully get your approval…

I Am More Likely Too Aggressively Seek Your Disapproval.

As well as look for any excuse to eject you out of my World.

I also am prone to bouts of frustration and contempt for those I despise (new product junkies, those with no character to stick with anything, quitters, and the list goes on). I cannot be bought or paid for. I refuse to sell to anyone after a deadline and am quick to drop entire businesses (like a wildly successful podcast I launched, or the popular elBenbo's Lair Facebook group I mentioned) if it doesn't fit my goals and lifestyle. I also am far more likely to try to *repel* you than attract you — for reasons I will explain in a later elBenbo Press Rule of Order about leaders versus experts. And the list goes on and on and on.

Now, the point of explaining this is not for you to copy me.

If you think that, congrats on missing the point, Maynard.

The Point Is for You to Create *Your* Own World.

With your own laws, rules, limitations, doors, and ways of doing business that go perfectly with *your* personality, skill sets, attributes, desires, preferences — all in a way that set you apart from anyone else's business (including *my* business). That is why **World-Building is all art, and zero science**. There is no magical checklist for doing it. It's pure intuition and instinct. It's something you build over time. Just like C.S. started with nothing but an image in his head of a faun in the forest and built his world from there… you start with one offer, build onto that, then build onto that, then build onto that. It is *not* something you do overnight. I say this so you don't let this intimidate you. You start with your own internal beliefs and attitudes and your personality, and a strong desire to right a wrong you see and build your World around that. Over time if you do it right, your World takes on a life of its own as you add, mix and match, and *stack* various different media platforms to get people into your World, buy your offers, and stay in perpetual contact with those people via the aggressive use of email marketing.

World-Building Is the Beating Heart of elBenbo Press.

You cannot skip this step if you want to use my ways.

You must embrace this step, work hard at it, and make it a way of life for you as you build your publishing business. It's the key to the whole game. And the best part is, you can start doing it today, and it doesn't cost you anything. All it takes is a shift in how you look at your business — as a "World" and not just a mere "business." Once people come inside your World, making sales to them becomes easy and automatic vs a constant struggle and chore trying to gamify and manipulate. It's a place people want to be and not a place you need to desperately try to keep people inside. It's a *privilege* to be in your World, not a right. It's an adventure from their boring lives. And, yes, it's…

A Platform Which is 100% You.

In essence, you become your own Platform.

A Platform that — even after your death, if you do it correctly — can never be truly cancelled, de-platformed, suppressed, manipulated, or controlled by Google or Facebook or any other big tech or government entity.

Bottom line:

This theme of World-Building will pop up over and over in this book.

And I will be showing you how to intertwine it with your elBenbo Press-driven business as we go forth. So, if this is still a bit murky, worry ye not. For now, I wanted to merely introduce you to this first and most important rule of the 9 elBenbo Press Rules of Order. As for *how* to start your business (or work it into your *existing* business) with World-Building already "baked" in, that's where elBenbo Press Rule of Order #2 comes in…

Appendix Three
–
World-Build Sociologically Not Psychologically

Another passage from my elBenbo Press book about World-Building. Again, to be notified next time this book is on sale, make sure you're on my daily email list at:

www.BenSettle.com

When I published the milestone 100th *Email Players* issue in November 2019 — about the six "money bombs" I'd used to explode sales higher than ever during the first 8 years of the newsletter's existence — I ended it with this zinger:

Before we wrap this issue up, a confession:

> **Originally when I decided to write about this topic, I had a seventh money-bomb to share. But I am holding off on sharing it for a while. I don't tell you this to tease or annoy you. I tell you this because I realized as I started writing about it, it's too big for just a section of a newsletter and deserves more space. So next year I will be writing about it in great detail and giving it the space and time it deserves. Frankly, it may even become its own book, or a big section of a book, I want to write about my publishing model. We will see. But the gist of it is, there are two kinds of business-building. And the one you hear from direct response marketers about tracking and testing metrics, sales, LTV (lifetime value), etc., while 100% correct, is less than half the picture, in my experience. There is another "intangible" side to things. And it's less psychological than it is *sociological* in the grand scheme things. And when you understand it, see examples of it, and start implementing what**

I am cryptically referring to… it can mean the difference between doing 5 figures and 6 figures, 6 figures and 7 figures, and probably 7 figures and 8 figures. It's a huge topic, but extremely important. And if it interests you to know more, stay tuned.

Following is that info I cut out.

And it's not only directly related to World-Building, but it's the engine that drives business World-Building. Plus, like World-Building, I'd been doing it for years already. But it wasn't until recently I was able to verbalize it, consciously do it, and — as of *this* book — teach it.

A quick story to set the stage:

If you were a fan of the *Game of Thrones* TV show, chances are (if you're like most of the fans, at least) you were underwhelmed at best by the last season. And, also if you are like most fans, you were very likely *outraged* by it at worst. Fans of the show know of what I speak on this. The show runners demonstrated a complete lack of respect for the fans 'intelligence, devotion, and years invested watching that show over its first seven seasons. I won't go into details about it here. But if you watched the last season especially, you probably felt…

Something was "off" about It.

Characters behaved in completely idiotic and non-consistent ways. Major, integral storylines long built up over seven seasons were ignored and abandoned. Virtue-Signaling to feminists and other assorted shrieking social media SJWs demanding "wokeness" was implemented at the expense of the overall story. Plotlines were rushed, if finished at all. Beloved characters were crapped on to the point where even the actors (you could tell if you watched any of their interviews) were disappointed and horrified by it, some even admitted to outright crying about it from dedicating years of their lives building a show that has virtually zero re-watchability now. And, of course, a thick, impenetrable suit of plot armor was put around characters who should have, by all rights, been killed off from the sheer magnitude of the threat and those characters 'realistically not living through it.

The reasons for this were many.

But do you know what the main reason is?

Well, it goes beyond mere convergence, with the writers wanting to force the plot and situations to virtue signal or place eye candy over substance and appease certain (small, but vocal) segments of the fanbase. Yes, those were a part of it. But what drove their decisions, the inept storytelling, and the overall miserable experience for fans (and the actors) the world over is…

They Shifted from George R.R. Martin's *Sociological* Storytelling Structure to Hollywood's Typical *Psychological* Storytelling Structure.

The tl:dr version of what this means is at:

https://blogs.scientificamerican.com/observations/the-real-reason-fans-hate-the-last-season-of-game-of-thrones

(**Note:** URLs come and go, and I have no control over it — thus, you'll have to search for it elsewhere if the above link is no longer working)

The article is very long but fascinating. But the important part as far as we are concerned here is this:

> **GOT was a beast as rare as a friendly dragon in King's Landing: it was sociological and institutional storytelling in a medium dominated by the psychological and the individual. This structural storytelling era of the show lasted through the seasons when it was based on the novels by George R. R. Martin, who seemed to specialize in having characters evolve in response to the broader institutional settings, incentives and norms that surround them. After the show ran ahead of the novels, however, it was taken over by powerful Hollywood showrunners David Benioff and D. B. Weiss. Some fans and critics have been assuming that the duo changed the narrative to fit Hollywood tropes or to speed things up, but that's unlikely. In fact, they probably stuck to the narrative points that were given to them, if only in outline form, by the original author. What they did is something different, but in many ways more fundamental: Benioff and Weiss steer the narrative lane away from the sociological and shifted to the psychological. That's the main, and often only, way Hollywood and most television writers tell stories.**

Here's the money-quote:

> **"...sociological and institutional storytelling in a medium dominated by the psychological and the individual."**

This is well worth the read, if you are a GOT fan. But, it is also vital you at least understand this in order to correctly implement the elBenbo Press publishing model, too. It is also directly related to the unsolicited advice-doling Mr. Metrics Guy I mentioned earlier. Like virtually every single direct response marketing book or program or course or seminar or training or "guru" advises — he created his business and runs his business from a *psychological* vantage point much like the GOT writers and other Hollywood storytellers create scripts.

In other words:

Instead of creating a sociological framework for a business (like Apple, Disney, etc., did) and leading his market... Mr. Metric Guy's decisions, product line, and overall business goals are dominated by the psychology of the customer and the offer. Thus, he lets all his metrics, tests, tracking data and what his market tells him to do dictate his business. If his metrics say one thing is no longer working, he switches it up to go where the metrics say to go.

Let me be very clear:

There is nothing wrong with doing this. In fact, this *psychological* way of building a business is a very smart and much safer way to go in my opinion, than the sociological way of building a business — and ultimately leading versus always reacting — used by Walt Disney, William Randolph Hearst, Steve Jobs, or other businesses that started off as one person's vision for wanting to right a wrong, and grew to billions as a result. And if you study any hardcore direct marketing teachers, gurus, and "legends" of the industry, chances are...

They All Teach and Insist on Psychological Business-Building Too.

For them it's all about the *numbers*.

And tests.

And metrics.

And data — from all their market research, carefully crafted and analyzed surveys, split tests, swipe file observations, being a marketing spy watching what others are doing that is currently working, and so on, and so forth.

Again, there is nothing "wrong" about doing any of that. It is, frankly, what more or less has built just about all the best, most successful, and wealthiest direct response businesses in history.

Or did it?

While I cannot speak for a single one of these teachers or business owners, I have noticed if you look at what they themselves do...

It's Sometimes the Exact Opposite of What They Teach!

In other words:

They engage — at least in part — in sociological, *not* psychological, business-building. Their own businesses are built upon a *framework* they created, and they let that framework dictate where it goes from there, rather than the data they may or may not even be tracking — even as they insist everyone else do just that. If you don't believe me, look at virtually any legitimately smart and well-known direct response marketing teacher, "guru", or author. I am going on pure observation. But from what I can see, many of them will tell you about tracking metrics, and numbers, and lifetime value, and running endless tests (and hardly anyone they teach this stuff to has enough traffic or leads to get a statistically relevant result, which alone tells you something in the milk ain't clean…) as a way of guiding their decisions and what to do next.

But, if you look at their *individual* businesses, I argue you will see very little of that.

On the contrary, what I see is…

Hardcore Sociological Business-Building.

There are very little true metrics involved.

And there is very little tracking of any kind — much less lifetime value data being collected or used. It's more like they created a framework first, and started with that, and not by running cold ads, generating leads via PPC or other paid advertising, calculating each person's lifetime value, etc. This is purely observational and I am leaving names out deliberately because I don't want to speak for anyone. Plus, it could be I am completely wrong about them anyway (I am not privy to anyone's internal marketing or data). But I can tell you just by observation that the big-name marketing teachers who I follow remind me an awful lot of what Walt Disney, or Steve Jobs, or William Randolph Hearst did after going through their biographies and examining their business structures. Almost all their decisions were ultimately based on *leading* their industries with a strongly-honed intuition, sharpened by knowing their markets, knowing human nature, and knowing what was coming down the pike.

They knew what offers their customers wanted to buy…

Before They Even Did!

Nobody asked for Snow White (Disney's first feature length animated film) or Disneyland, or the iPod, iPad, iPhone, etc., that Jobs pioneered.

Those were based on *leading* the market, not reacting to it.

To bring this back to the online marketing world, take a look at the great Sean D'Souza's business. I'll be talking a lot more about him later in this book. I don't know the internal data or workings of his business. But I do know he admitted at a *System Seminar* back in 2008 when explaining the eerily-sounding *sociological* framework for his own business:

"We don't use analytics or any of that and I don't have any data — I started out as a cartoonist and I moved to marketing and this has allowed us to take three vacations per year, buy houses, travel, do all the things we really wanted to do. We earn more money than we need."

Again, I can't speak for Sean.

But what he said and what he teaches about business-building (focusing on consumption — and not merely attraction and conversion, which is the only thing you hear any other marketing teacher talk about) is what I consider to be a *sociological* built business vs a psychologically built business. It's the way I have always run my business, too. Whether it's my elBenbo Press publishing business model or the SaaS business I have ownership in that my business partner Troy Broussard created — there are no focus groups, surveys, going blind looking at tracking and click data, or any of that.

It's more a matter of starting with an overall right to wrong, or a pain to alleviate, or a desire to help people achieve, and then...

Letting That Dictate What is Sold.

Not testing and tracking.

Not surveys and following what my competitors are doing.

And certainly not asking and soliciting what my customers want.

There is wisdom in looking at what your market is *already* buying, and starting off with that. I have done that myself, and still would to guide me on any new business ventures. But after that it's about leading and directing your market and customers, not reacting and being directed by them. This goes back to the beginning of this section. Every word of the email I wrote explaining how not a single person ever outright asked for any of the books I sell is true. In fact, I don't think it is any accident the ones that I sold on pure gut instinct and intuition alone (my *Villains* books and *Brand Barbarian* book specifically)...

Are Some of the Highest-Selling Books I Ever Launched.

I'll show how to get this "sixth sense" later (via "chi sau" with your list).

But for now, I simply want to introduce you to the idea of sociological business-building vs psychological business-building. Psychological business-building is running ads, doing customer surveys, analyzing market data, and then building your offers around that information, first. Again, it's a much safer way to do it than sociological business-building: which is the opposite — starting with an overall wrong you want to right or problem to solve, and then leading your market via building your offers around that, first. This means creating and running your business by creating a "World" and letting the "characters" (your market, customers, leads, offers, etc.) organically work inside that World, rather than letting cold, hard metrics dictate what offers you create, who you sell to, etc. In my business, a lot of it is gut feeling and instinct based on *experience* and what I know of the kind of customers I want to serve. It's also having a vision of what I want to do and where I want to go, and then letting my business grow organically from that. Thus, I create offers within the World I am creating, rather than around what my market is asking for. Nobody but nobody (and certainly it had nothing to do with hard data, analytics, or metrics) asked for *Copy Slacker Copy Troll, Infotainment Jackpot, Affiliate Launch Copynomicon*, my *Villains books* or even *Email Players*... or any of the successful products I sell. A case could be made for my *Email Players List Swell* book. But even that was built not to offer something anyone asked for, but because I got sick of people asking me about list building (not my strong suit)...

And I Wanted to Shut Them Up.

I even admit as such in the sales letter.

My business is not built on asking anyone if they want anything. Instead, I simply built a framework, know the challenges my list and market face, and let my business grow from there. If you look closely, you'll see this is also how Howard Stern built his empire. It's even how Donald Trump got elected in 2016 against all odds — ignoring all his so-called advisors and rigged poll numbers, and instead speaking from the gut and following the exact same kind of framework he's used to build businesses vs the poll-driven politics of virtually all other politicians relying on advisors and number crunching.

Now, contrast that to just a "by the numbers business."

Like, for example, Mr. Metrics Guy who was horrified I would not let him buy. Why I would not send out an offer to get people who have quit *Email Players* (who I want nothing to do with — based on how I want to run my business, not what the market tells me to do) to get them to re-subscribe. Why I would not have a money-back guarantee. Why I would not plaster my advertising with testimonials. Why I would not just re-use the same emails that "worked" over and over but also re-use emails that did not initially "work." (Hint: many times, emails that did not make a lot of sales the first time they ran, do make a lot of sales the second time I use them — which is a whole other topic in and of itself...). Why I would not use Google or other testing software to measure every click, opt-in, and sale (especially lifetime value), and then parse that all via a spreadsheet that dictates what comes next... and the list goes on.

Again, I'm not saying any of that is "wrong."

In a lot of ways, it's the safe way to go.

But I will also say that, in my experience…

Building and Running Your Business Psychologically Is Nowhere Near as Fun, Satisfying, and Potentially Profitable as Building and Running Your Business Sociologically.

A psychologically directed business doesn't care about or utilize principles like customer curation, or purposely making yourself more scarce to make yourself more valuable, fully using self-aggrandizement, being a personality-driven brand, killing off profitable products or services because it's no longer fun, selling what you know your market needs rather than only selling what they say and even have demonstrated what they want, and the list goes on. Those are all part and parcel of a sociologically built and directed business. And they are the exact opposite of building everything upon analytics, metrics, measurability, testing, only selling what they are already buying, etc. I keep saying building your business psychologically is much safer, and maybe even smarter for the majority. And you can grow a very big company doing it. So, I don't bring this up to take a dump on the psychological way of building a business. I bring this up because if you want to use the elBenbo Press publishing model, you must build your business *sociologically*, not psychologically. Everything else you will read in this book is predicated and dependent on both this and World-Building.

In other words:

It's About the Leadership, Framework, and Relationships First, and the Offers, Metrics, and Transactions Second.

You create a World, you fill it with characters (offers) that right a wrong in your market's life, and you lead, not react to the market. If you launch an insanely successful offer, but it doesn't go with your World, you kill it off (like I did with the wildly successful podcast & Facebook group I mentioned). For example, if you know your market will be better served giving them a way to run their business from the palms of their hands versus having to "Frankenstein" together a business with VAs, multiple Wordpress/cloud platforms/media distribution sites, etc., you offer it to them (like we did with our *Learnistic* mobile app platform). If you see a "hole" in your product line that can make all your other products more effective for your customers regardless of them asking for it or not, you create it and offer it (as I did with my *Villains books* and my *Brand Barbarian, Copy Troll*, and *Infotainment Jackpot* books). *In sociological storytelling the characters are vital and important, they don't dictate the story, nor is the story dependent on any one of them living or not being killed off. In sociological business-building the offers are vital and important, but they don't dictate the business.*

Nor Is the Business Dependent on Any
One of the Offers Being Successful.

It's about the framework, vision, and leadership.

This is the difference between creating a "great character" who builds a suit of armor or creating the Marvel Cinematic Universe. Or between creating a "great computer" or building a multi-media business like Apple that is also in the phone, music, and cloud business. Or the difference between creating a "great menu" or building McDonalds or In-N-Out Burger — each with their own rules, cultures, and ways of doing business that are the exact opposite of each other in many ways. If Marvel kills off Ironman (which they did), the cinematic universe still goes on. If McDonalds decided to end the Big Mac, the franchise would still move forward. And if Apple stopped selling computers or Disney stopped making animated films (which they did for over a decade, at one time) altogether, their company would still keep growing.

And the reason why is sociological business-building.

Like World-Building, sociological business-building is a theme that will run throughout this entire book. They are also both vital for understanding and applying this next part that follows.

World-Building!

This is an admittedly weird branding technique. And virtually nobody does it, much less understands it. But the inspiration for this is the late, great Gary Gygax who went from being a small-town cobbler to inventing *Dungeons & Dragons* in his basement. And he was responsible in many ways for the entire billion dollar RPG (role playing game) industry. His work also became the template and inspiration for everything from computer RPGs to popular hit shows like *Game Of Thrones*. Anyway, all those hours of mindlessly playing *Dungeons & Dragons* growing up were put to good and profitable use. Turns out, I had spent years of my life learning World-Building via "osmosis" and without even realizing it. And, later, when I started writing my novels I continued to learn and feel my way through building my own worlds. In fact, shortly before creating my group, a chick from a big New York company that match-makes writers with editors and big publishers emailed me saying she loved the World-Building in my *Enoch Wars* novels and would like to help me out. But, since I was strictly self-published I declined. Still, she was the one that got me thinking even more about World-Building. And so, with elBenbo's Lair I very deliberately built a "world" out of it — a society — and not a typical group for people to come and share value, articles, or tips. In fact, a couple years before even founding elBenbo's Lair I was inspired to build my own "world" in the business community after reading some *Kick Ass* comics, and noticing the writer Mark Millar has done just that with his brand. I even do some periodic inserts (inspired by him) where I tell my *Email Players* subscribers what is going on in my world besides the stuff they see in my daily emails, products, newsletter, etc.

Anyway, back to World-Building:

Each time I built a Thread-hole (a thread of comments and rabid back-and-forth interaction, debate, etc.) I treated it like its own *Dungeons & Dragons* module — complete with unexpected twists, turns, and even character deaths (like when someone would get so offended or fed up with my antics they'd leave elBenbo's Lair or I'd blacklist them for breaking my No-Value rule). This was all planned and worked out over time. elBenbo's Lair had its own language (we even had a Lexicon), culture, customs, borders, trade with other groups (I often plugged other peoples' groups — and vice versa). In that world, I picked fights (more like, gave people options for thinking differently, I rarely ever debated or argued, although I did if I see saw injustice going on inside its borders — like any leader of society would). I built a harem of women (there was a very *90210* and soap opera-like subculture going on I did deliberately, being inspired by the late producer Aaron Spelling's World-Building). I had a cast of characters, a Main Chick, a Concubine, a Side Chick, a Booty Call, A Grim Reaper, and some Minions, as well as an "Inner Circle" (the only ones who were allowed to give value), and a HBIC (Head Bitch In Charge) — all satire and infotainment, of course. I also even had a "Scribe" who kept track of all the Thread-holes and summarized them each night. And the list goes on.

Anyway, here's the point:

This was a very carefully built world. Others had tried to duplicate it but they simply couldn't. And the reason why they couldn't was because I combined World-Building with my unique Personality to create a Brand of its own. It's something I had been doing already to my email list, and applied it to Facebook, and nowadays I do it even more deliberately.

You can, too, and without doing all the zany things I did.

Here's how:

1. Curate with Extreme Prejudice — including your time, your friends, your fans, your customers, your JV/business partners, your clients, and everything else in your business. By "curate" I mean be extremely selective about who you allow to buy from you, who you allow to be on your email list, who you follow on social media (and who you allow to follow you on social media), who you listen to, who you ignore, what emails you answer or don't answer, who you will take calls from, and the list goes on. Call it hate and prejudice if you want against those I know make terrible customers or who annoy, frustrate, or waste my time, but it is what it is. I have contempt for them as customers (not as people, necessarily, context…), thus I curate them out. And if you want a rock-solid brand, then create a business where only the best, cream-of-the-crop customers are around you, referring to you, and associating with you. I am absolutely ruthless about this. And the more ruthless I get about this, the stronger my brand gets, the better my customer base gets, and the bigger my profits get. In some ways, it creates a brand that has almost no choice but to attract hordes of new business over time… even when I might screw other things up sometimes in my marketing. In my own case — and your curation will differ — I only answer non-customer service questions from *Email Players* subscribers. I am quick to jettison subscribers who ask stupid questions they could find on Google or who waste my time, try to create drama (who I especially loathe), or require too much handholding. I only cater to people who are not price shoppers, who have real businesses, and who are deeper, long-term, and investment-minded people, as opposed to new product junkies (i.e. people who are addicted to the dopamine drip they get when they buy something new — they are horrible customers who do nothing with what I teach them, and have very little discipline or financial self-control, I want nothing to do with them) and do-nothings just playing business.

All of Which Cultivates a Very Distinct, and Clearly-Defined Brand.

A brand that is not easily copied or ripped off.

It horrifies those who hate being rejected, and turns them into trolls sometimes (which I happily add to my Narrative). But when it comes to business I am exclusive due to my curation. And the more exclusive I get, the stronger my brand gets, the bigger my business gets, and the more abundant my joy at doing business gets. And no, you don't have to do any of the above exactly as I do. In fact, if your personality is not like mine and your goals are different than mine, doing so would be dishonest and inauthentic, inconsistent, and you'd come off as extremely needy the harder you try to posture otherwise. I want to be very clear here: When I am talking about curation, *it has to be in 100% congruence with "you", and not based on me or anyone else*. In other words, curate, don't duplicate.

2. Create your own lexicon — This is also Matt Furey 101, where you invent your own words, over time, that people start to associate with you and your brand. But it's also got a much deeper history to it starting with the late J.R.R. Tolkien. The main genius behind his *Lord of the Rings* books — still the #1 books in the epic fantasy genre, and always probably will be — is because he invented his own languages, using his education in linguistics. That gave the world, characters, and stories he created far more depth, and created a far more passionate fanbase than other authors.

But notice I said invent *your* own language. You don't have to be a professor of languages to tap into this powerful branding technique. It's way too easy — which is why so many people who can't think for themselves do it — to just lift words you see invented by someone else and then try to pass them off as your own. ***The more you sound like someone else, the weaker your brand is***. But invent doesn't mean whole cloth. You can take unique words from pop culture and apply them to your business. I sometimes take words from obscure movies or books, for example. Or just change the way common words are spelled. Thus, in my business, back in 2009 I invented words like goo-roo, bewbs, ex-spurt, gluteus assimus, etc. You can not only start using this info as soon as you learn it, but you can potentially profit from it very quickly, too. Start creating words and your own "language" immediately and use them.

3. Make rules for doing business with you — this goes back to curation, but the more rules and barriers you erect for being able to buy from you, sell to you, and do business with you at all, the stronger your brand will likely be if you do it right.

I did this especially aggressively in my old Facebook group.

Like, for example, a No-Value rule (nobody but me and my Inner Circle were allowed to give value). Or my stringent Immigration policy (if someone was in too many other groups, I banned them from mine). Or my no troll rule, and the list goes on. In my business now, I have rules like I don't allow anyone with the word "swipe" in their email address to subscribe to my list. I don't do business with anyone who asks about a refund policy (not that I have a refund policy, but I already know the mentality someone who asks has — as they are telling you exactly what they intend to do). I don't let trolls or people who ask questions based on their own emotional baggage buy from me. And I don't allow people who cancel their *Email Players* subscriptions come back later.

And the list goes on and on and on.

Again, you don't have to do any of these things — and probably you shouldn't, depending on your personality and business goals.

The point here is to have a very specific and deliberately created set of rules for doing business with you and buying from you. Not only does this strengthen your brand and curate your customers so you only deal with the ones you want, but it gives you more peace of mind, a more solid business, and builds credibility — since **the more barriers you put up, the more credibility you have**. (A down-n-dirty and low tech tip for building rock-solid credibility to tuck away in your mind, that I first heard from the great Dan Kennedy.) And the more you draw lines, have standards, and enforce rules in your business, the bigger, stronger, and more profitable your brand should become over time.

4. Always look out for your audience's best interests via "sticking hands" — even if, and especially if, it comes at your own financial expense. This means don't skimp on service. Do the little things that will make their experience not just good, but *great*. And constantly be in contact with your market (daily email is best for this, in my opinion) so you get a sense for what they want before they even do. This is one of the single most profitable things you can ever do for your business, and one of the single most effective things you can ever do for your brand.

The analogy I like to use is from Wing Chun kung fu:

In Wing Chun, you are constantly learning how to feel and interpret force. Your physical attributes (size, strength, speed, eyesight, etc.) are not nearly as important as being able to feel what someone is going to do before they even do it. This is what lets ancient kung fu masters who are old, slow, weak, and not nearly as powerful as they were in their youth still trounce younger, stronger, faster, and more powerful opponents — because they can feel what someone is going to do before they do it. They use their eyes, yes. But, they don't trust them. The eyes are very slow compared to touch and tactile feel

— which is instant, and always accurate. In Wing Chun you train how to interpret force like this via what's called Chi Sau, or:

"Sticking Hands"

This is where you and your partner train in a way where you are constantly in contact and trying to get the upper hand by focusing on feeling what the other person is going to do. Very fascinating stuff, and very profitable, too, if you know how to apply it to business.

Take surveys, for example.

I remember reading in Ken McCarthy's magnificent tome *The System Club Letters* how The GAP made a huge blunder a few years back by relying on surveys to make their decisions (asking people what they want) instead of going by the instinct (i.e. interpretation of force) created by all their knowledge of their customers, buying trends, sales figures, and overall observations about their market honed from years of selling to them.

The result?

Sales Plummeted!

And their brand naturally took a big hit. All because they trusted their surveys (i.e., their eyes which are slow and deceptive). When, what they should have been trusting is their knowledge of what their customers and market like to buy. (i.e., their tactile interpretation of force).

Here are some more examples:

When I created my *Copy Slacker* book, not a single person asked me to create it. There was no human cry for it or demand for it from my list. Nobody said, "Ben please create a comprehensive copywriting methodology I can learn in just a few hours, that covers everything I need to know, and that is great for slackers!" In fact, I don't think a single person ever asked me to create a copywriting product at all.

But I knew they wanted one.

How?

Because of constant *daily* email contact with my list. Every time I mail my list I get feedback in the form of comments, questions, what they are buying from me (and what they are *not* buying), and so on, and so forth. This information lets me know what they want, without them ever outright telling me. And many people have asked questions, for example, about other peoples' courses, have told me what they struggle with, and ranted about all the things that frustrate them about copywriting. All this comes from their gut, and out of honesty. No survey could have given me this info without skewed and biased results. But I never need one anyway, because I am in constant contact with my list. Every day of the year. Thus, when I launched it, hardly anyone even read the sales letter. Maybe a few people did. But, going by the responses I got by email, on flakebook, etc, I am convinced well over 70% of the people who bought (and it was the biggest launch I'd ever done to my own list at the time) did it...

Sight Unseen!

They knew they wanted it.

And, in many cases I found out, they wanted it *before* they even knew they did. That's the power of building your own world and creating a brand via daily emails (i.e., sticking hands). You can do the same on social media with daily interaction. But it's not nearly as effective, in my experience, as doing it via email.

Another example:

Not one single bloke ever asked me to write a book about the persuasion secrets of the world's most influential and charismatic villains. Yet, my *Villains* books have been some of the biggest book launches I've ever created — and without any drama queening, affiliates, social media hype, or joint ventures. And even now, all three volumes sell whenever I merely mention it, with tons of word-of-mouth about it due to the brand I've curated and cultivated and created via mailing daily, interpreting what my market wants via their feedback, reading between the lines of what they say, and noting their questions or comments or complaints or praise.

One final example:

The folks at AWAI.com told me my *10-Minute Workday* program was the single biggest launch they ever did at that time. (And that's saying something!) And the irony is: One of their biggest draws is showing copywriters how to get freelance clients. Yet my program with them, and the sales letter, and theme of the promotion, is *client-less* copywriting: how to create your own copywriting business so you don't need clients. To my knowledge, nobody asked them to create a program about this. But they knew, because they are in constant contact with their file, and knew exactly what they wanted without having to ask them. There have been many other products created like this, too (all my books, in fact) — each based on my unique list's desires. And what amuses me most is, these product ideas don't work for my copycats who try to create their own versions, because they have not taken the time to find out not only what their meager audiences will buy before they even know... but don't have the brand that makes it "safe" to buy experimental products like the kind I create in my "world", that I keep building upon.

This is why strictly adhering to the three Brand Barbarian rules are vital. And it's also why...

All Those "Me Too!" Copycat Brands Are So Weak.

Moral of the story: Constant, consistent, and relentless contact with your list, your market, and your customers can build you a powerful brand people buy from, and often sight-unseen, simply because you have such a strong sense of what they want before they even do. It not only builds a unique brand and world of your own, but can add many thousands, hundreds of thousands, even potentially millions of dollars to your hog nasty piggy bank over the lifespan of your business.

5. Recruit within your fan base — there are many advantages to this and very few (if any) disadvantages. By recruit from your fan base, I am talking about, whenever possible, hire employees, assistants, designers, coders, writers, lawyers, etc., who are not just good at what they do... and who are not just customers... but *fans*. I do this whenever possible. And each time, I am amazed at how much more loyal those fans are, how much more they refer, and how much more seriously they take assignments and jobs than those who are not fans. There are many reasons for this, like, for example, fans have your back, and are on your side. They are usually familiar with your personality and ways of doing things. They obviously like you or they wouldn't be fans. They also tend to be far more loyal, and...

Have Far More Respect for What You Are Doing, and for Your Mission, than Some Random Service You Pick or Are Referred To.

More:

Doing this also can add tremendously to your brand, as their other clients and customers start to associate you with them and vice versa, strengthening and enhancing both of your brands and bringing more buyers into both your worlds — effectively letting you "siphon" hundreds of new customers from each other over time. I have found this with my web master, my graphic designer, my editor, my transcriptionist, and the list goes on. I have even applied this to my romantic relationships — yes recruiting from your fanbase can save you a lot of time, and does what PUA's call "pre-selects" women for you if you are a man. (No idea how that works for chicks.) i.e., just like customers feel safe doing business with people other businesses and people they like and trust do business with, many times women like to know a man is wanted by other women first before dating them.

There are many more things you can do to build a powerful brand via World-Building. But this should give you plenty to work on. And if you did nothing but master these, your brand will have almost no choice but to become not just good, but truly great. And, quite literally, a *world* all its own...

Appendix Five

—

World War Mobile

Transcript excerpt about World-Building and the ever-growing mobile app technology available to direct response marketers and other businesses. For more about this kind of technology, and how to use it affordably check out:

www.EmailPlayers.com/learnistic

TOM BEAL: Y'all have touched on so many valid and important points. If I'm putting myself in the shoes of the people that are here from and looking to see *Learnistic Pro* as a tool for them, and A, most of them came here and are listening to this from a deep link. Troy, what you just mentioned, they're here, they experienced it. You've experienced that and now you can see how that was seamless, and as Troy mentioned, brought you right to the exact point.

Now, as Troy just mentioned, 87% of his buyers were in the app and it's only less than 50% of his list. Not everybody's going to. from your email list, join you in the app, but these are your hyper engaged raving fan buyers who get to see behind the veil. And so, Ben, I'm going to circle back to you. You're the king of World-Building. How is this the ultimate world build for bringing your people out of the massive distractions that is online to bring them into your sole app fully focused? What's the benefits behind that World-Building?

BEN SETTLE: The app is one aspect of World-Building. It's not the only thing you do, but I mean, it is a huge part of it because that phone is with them. Now, I once saw this analogy because I really want everyone listening to understand where your customers are. Unless you happen to sell to people who are still using rotary phones or something, but we're not talking about them. We're talking about the average person. This analogy was so true when I saw it and I don't remember who said it, but I have to give the person props. She's like, "I read this section of *The Fellowship of the Ring* where Bilbo's talking…" You guys have all read Lord the Rings or seen the movies and

Bilbo 's talking about how he has to look at the Ring all the time. He's always checking in on it to make sure it's safe. It's like an eye always looking at him and watching him. A voice talking to him. He's always thinking about it. He brings it with him everywhere. He knows it has this hold on him.

This person says, "I just realized my phone is the One Ring of Power." This is really how attached the average person now is to their mobile phone. There's always going to be people, and I got to say this because we're going to hear from some idiot reply guy who's going to say, "Well, I don't use it. I don't use a phone. This is creepy." We're not talking about them. Let me be very clear. We're not talking about people who still use flip phones because they're afraid that Biden's going to come and send a Gestapo after them. We're not talking about that. We're talking about regular people.

They are attached to their phone in ways that some might even say are unhealthy. We are adding, unfortunately, Troy, God help us, to this problem. We may be judged for this someday. We are adding to the problem by introducing marketers to this type of thing. But this is where the World-Building comes in. See, World-Building really isn't anything new. It's been around for I don't know how long. Certainly, role playing games made it a thing and epic fantasy has made it a thing. But really, it just comes down to building a place where people go to, and they don't want to leave. When they do leave, it's depressing to them.

Now, here's the example I'm going to give since we're talking about Lord of The Rings. This is from the Narnia books. If you haven't seen the movies, just try to follow along this. I don't know what to tell you. C.S. Lewis built this world called Narnia in the books. People find doorways into that world, especially the first two books where these kids find their way in. In the first book they find their way in, they have adventures. It's an interesting fascinating place. It's certainly more interesting and fascinating than the boring real world, where they're just kind of hanging out in this mansion with this old guy and they had nothing to do all day but get in trouble and they're doing nothing productive with their lives whatsoever. But they go into Narnia and they have all these adventures and they save the day and they become kings and queens in there and they are there for 15 years.

And so, one day, they get kicked out in Narnia abruptly. Now, their whole journey in life is to get back to Narnia to talk about Narnia, to think about Narnia, to want to experience it and to trade stories about it. One of the characters, Susan, she ends up becoming very bitter about it and starts making fun of her siblings and says, "Yeah, we sure had fun as kids, but time to grow up and all that." She's not even allowed back. She'd be like the today's version of a troll, who trolls you. You just kick them out and they can't come back. I'm telling you, this is the kind of thing if you understand how to build a world, this is how it is.

Social media lets you play this very well if you know how to do it, email does—especially BerserkerMail—and now, mobile app technology because you can absolutely build a world. I've been doing this with my fiction. You can ask Daniel Throssell, for example. He just wrote an intro for one of my novels and I put it in the app. The Great Bob Bly, sent me an intro for one of my novels. I put it in the app. I have videos in the app. I have interviews in the app. I have things talking about fiction and writing and the world I've built in the app.

People who are interested in that go in there and they're just in there going around and they're on their phone and they're thinking about it and they're interacting with it and they're engaging with me even though it's not a one-on-one type of engagement. They're engaging with my mind. They're engaging with concepts and ideas and philosophies and things that I have espoused. I can do this via email. I can do this I guess if I was on Facebook, and I have I had a very, very rabid Facebook group at one time that was probably one of the most engaged in my entire niche and that helped.

But ultimately, that was somebody else's brand. That was Facebook. There were distractions in there that I could not get around and that annoyed people because they wanted to be in my world. Email's the same way. You're not the only person in the inbox, but this mobile app aspect, if they're in your app, they're in your app. They're not really getting a lot of distraction. They might get a push notification or something, but they're in there. It's not like a website, which is very easy to click away from. If you have some content in there like an audio or a video or a PDF or whatever, an article, they're on their phone in your world engaging with your world. They're in your Narnia if you're doing it right. They're in your middle earth if you're doing it right. And they won't want to leave, if you do it right. And when they do, they'll only think about getting back in.

If you understand how to build that connection, why would they want to go anywhere? They'll probably be in your app more than anywhere else. I mean, that's the goal. Again, I'm an email guy. I'm a print newsletter guy. I'm a physical book guy, but I cannot build that connection as precise as I can with a mobile app. Again, I'm just getting started with this myself. It's a fascinating thing and Learnistic Pro is going to help dial that up even more.

For more info on Learnistic mobile app technology go to:
www.EmailPlayers.com/learnistic

Appendix Four
–
World-Building for World-Domination!

This is a bit from my best-selling book *Brand Barbarian* talking about World-Building from a branding point of view. Like the other books mentioned in these appendices, to be notified next time this book is on sale, make sure you're on my daily email list at:

www.BenSettle.com

Once upon a time, I had what I believe was one of the most rabidly-engaged and addictive Facebook groups (called *elBenbo's Lair*) in my niche. And I mean that literally — as people would complain about it being so addictive to the point where they had so many posts inside showing up on their main feed, they often would post things publicly (including things they didn't want to be seen by friends and family) thinking they were posting in the group. It was a group that had been mocked, laughed at, awed at, angered at, loved on, and, yes, a huge profit source for certain people within its walls. My group (or, Society, as I called it, it was way more than just a mere group) broke nearly every rule a Facebook group is supposed to follow. Especially according to the Facebook fluffpreneurs always prattling on about "engagement" and "authority" and "value" and whatever other trendy buzz words they spew out when making videos in their cars or in a hotel in Bali. Many tried to copy elBenbo's Lair, but quickly found it could not be duplicated. And it did more for my brand than almost any other thing (including my daily emails, which it worked hand-in-hand with) I was doing at the time. The only reason I closed it was because it was getting too rabid for me to keep up with, and a huge distraction of internet drama, and stopped being fun.

Whatever the case, there were many reasons for its success. But, the first and most important reason — especially when it comes to branding — was I engaged in the mysterious and exciting craft of:

Appendix Six

–

World-Building Inspiration and Resource Library

Ray Harryhausen: *Special Effects Titan*

Dungeons & Dragons Art & Arcana: A Visual History Dungeons & Dragons A Visual History—by Witwer, Michael, Newman, Kyle, Peterson, Jon, Witwer, Sam, Official Dungeons & Dragons Licensed, et al.

Eye of the Beholder: The Art of Dungeons and Dragons

The Art of Todd McFarlane: The Devil's in the Details—by Todd McFarlane

Walt Disney: Triumph of the American Imagination—by Neal Gabler

Writing for Comics and Graphic Novels—by Peter David

Rise of the Dungeon Master: Gary Gygax and the Creation of D&D Rise of the Dungeon Master—by David Kushner and Koren Shadmi

Empire of Imagination: Gary Gygax and the Birth of Dungeons & Dragons—by Michael Witwer

Stan Lee's Mutants, Monsters & Marvels

Chris Claremont's *X-Men*

The Lord of the Rings trilogy—by J.R.R. Tolkien

The Chronicles of Narnia—by C.S. Lewis

Arkhaven Comics—by Vox Day

Writing for Comics and Graphic Novels—by Peter David

Steve Jobs—by Walter Isaacson

Early Marvel Comics titles written by Stan Lee and Chris Claremont (*X-Men* titles Chris wrote, especially)

Bandersnatch: C.S. Lewis, J.R.R. Tolkien, and the Creative Collaboration of the Inklings—by Diana Pavlac Glyer

Fantastic Paintings of Frazetta—by J. David Spurlock

Avengers: Earth's Mightiest Heroes—a great example of how to approach and structure World-Building. Watch the first season. Note how it starts with one hero and one villain, then methodically tacks on more detail, more depth, more foreshadowing of what's to come, and more heroes or villains or characters coming and going, interacting, "crossing over," and all working towards various storylines and one cohesive World. It's a great "template" for World-Building if you pay attention and look at your offers as characters and take the World-Building sections of this book seriously. Also, as a sidebar, the context of that show is it came out a couple years before the Avengers movie, making it a sort of "sales pitch" for that big event in many ways. All of this is directly applicably to building an elBenbo Press publishing business.

World of Legal Jargon

All trademarks and service marks are the properties of their respective owners. All references to these properties are made solely for editorial purposes. Except for marks actually owned by the Author or the Publisher, no commercial claims are made to their use, and neither the Author nor the Publisher is affiliated with such marks in any way. Unless otherwise expressly noted, none of the individuals or business entities mentioned herein has endorsed the contents of this book.

Limits of Liability & Disclaimers of Warranties

Because this book is a general educational information product, it is not a substitute for professional advice on the topics discussed in it. The materials in this book are provided "as is" and without warranties of any kind either express or implied. The Author and the Publisher disclaim all warranties, express or implied, including, but not limited to, implied warranties of merchantability and fitness for a particular purpose. The Author and the Publisher do not warrant that defects will be corrected, or that any website or any server that makes this book available is free of viruses or other harmful components. The Author does not warrant or make any representations regarding the use or the results of the use of the materials in this book in terms of their correctness, accuracy, reliability, or otherwise. Applicable law may not allow the exclusion of implied warranties, so the above exclusion may not apply to you.

Under no circumstances, including, but not limited to, negligence, shall the Author or the Publisher be liable for any special or consequential damages that result from the use of, or the inability to use this book, even if the Author, the Publisher, or an authorized representative has been advised of the possibility of such damages. Applicable law may not allow the limitation or exclusion of liability or incidental or consequential damages, so the above limitation or exclusion may not apply to you. In no event shall the Author or

Publisher total liability to you for all damages, losses, and causes of action (whether in contract, tort, including but not limited to, negligence or otherwise) exceed the amount paid by you, if any, for this book.

You agree to hold the Author and the Publisher of this book, principals, agents, affiliates, and employees harmless from any and all liability for all claims for damages due to injuries, including attorney fees and costs, incurred by you or caused to third parties by you, arising out of the products, services, and activities discussed in this book, excepting only claims for gross negligence or intentional tort.

You agree that any and all claims for gross negligence or intentional tort shall be settled solely by confidential binding arbitration per the American Arbitration Association's commercial arbitration rules. All arbitration must occur in the municipality where the Author's principal place of business is located. Arbitration fees and costs shall be split equally, and you are solely responsible for your own lawyer fees.

Facts and information are believed to be accurate at the time they were placed in this book. All data provided in this book is to be used for information purposes only. The information contained within is not intended to provide specific legal, financial, tax, physical or mental health advice, or any other advice whatsoever, for any individual or company and should not be relied upon in that regard. The services described are only offered in jurisdictions where they may be legally offered. Information provided is not all-inclusive, and is limited to information that is made available and such information should not be relied upon as all-inclusive or accurate.

For more information about this policy, please contact the Author at the e-mail address listed in the Copyright Notice at the front of this book.

IF YOU DO NOT AGREE WITH THESE TERMS AND EXPRESS CONDITIONS, DO NOT READ THIS BOOK. YOUR USE OF THIS BOOK, PRODUCTS, SERVICES, AND ANY PARTICIPATION IN ACTIVITIES MENTIONED IN THIS BOOK, MEAN THAT YOU ARE AGREEING TO BE LEGALLY BOUND BY THESE TERMS.

Affiliate Compensation and Material Connections Disclosure

This book may contain hyperlinks to websites and information created and maintained by other individuals and organizations. The Author and the Publisher do not control or guarantee the accuracy, completeness, relevance, or timeliness of any information or privacy policies posted on these linked websites.

You should assume that all references to products and services in this book are made because material connections exist between the Author or Publisher and the providers of the mentioned products and services ("Provider"). You should also assume that all hyperlinks within this book are affiliate links for (a) the Author, (b) the Publisher, or (c) someone else who is an affiliate for the mentioned products and services (individually and collectively, the "Affiliate").

The Affiliate recommends products and services in this book based in part on a good faith belief that the purchase of such products or services will help readers in general.

The Affiliate has this good faith belief because (a) the Affiliate has tried the product or service mentioned prior to recommending it or (b) the Affiliate has researched the reputation of the Provider and has made the decision to recommend the Provider's products or services based on the Provider's history of providing these or other products or services.

The representations made by the Affiliate about products and services reflect the Affiliate's honest opinion based upon the facts known to the Affiliate at the time this book was published.

Because there is a material connection between the Affiliate and Providers of products or services mentioned in this book, you should always assume that the Affiliate may be biased because of the Affiliate's relationship with a Provider and/or because the Affiliate has received or will receive something of value from a Provider.

Perform your own due diligence before purchasing a product or service mentioned in this book. The type of compensation received by the Affiliate may vary. In some instances, the Affiliate may receive complimentary products (such as a review copy), services, or money from a Provider prior to mentioning the Provider's products or services in this book.

In addition, the Affiliate may receive a monetary commission or non-monetary compensation when you take action by clicking on a hyperlink in this book. This includes, but is not limited to, when you purchase a product or service from a Provider after clicking on an affiliate link in this book.

Earnings & Income Disclaimers

No Earnings Projections, Promises or Representations

For purposes of these disclaimers, the term "Author" refers individually and collectively to the author of this book and to the affiliate (if any) whose affiliate links are embedded in this book.

You recognize and agree that the Author and the Publisher have made no implications, warranties, promises, suggestions, projections, representations or guarantees whatsoever to you about future prospects or earnings, or that you will earn any money, with respect to your purchase of this book, and that the Author and the Publisher have not authorized any such projection, promise, or representation by others.

Any earnings or income statements, or any earnings or income examples, are only estimates of what you might earn. There is no assurance you will do as well as stated in any examples. If you rely upon any figures provided, you must accept the entire risk of not doing as well as the information provided. This applies whether the earnings or income examples are monetary in nature or pertain to advertising credits which may be earned (whether such credits are convertible to cash or not).

There is no assurance that any prior successes or past results as to earnings or income (whether monetary or advertising credits, whether convertible to cash or not) will apply, nor can any prior successes be used, as an indication of your future success or results from any of the information, content, or strategies. Any and all claims or representations as to income or earnings (whether monetary or advertising credits, whether convertible to cash or not) are not to be considered as "average earnings."

Testimonials and Examples

Testimonials and examples in this book are exceptional results, do not reflect the typical purchaser's experience, do not apply to the average person and are not intended to represent or guarantee that anyone will achieve the same or similar results. Where specific income or earnings (whether monetary or advertising credits, whether convertible to cash or not), figures are used and attributed to a specific individual or business, that individual or business has earned that amount. There is no assurance that you will do as well using the same information or strategies. If you rely on the specific income or earnings figures used, you must accept all the risk of not doing as well. The described experiences are atypical. Your financial results are likely to differ from those described in the testimonials.

The Economy

The economy, where you do business, on a national and even worldwide scale, creates additional uncertainty and economic risk. An economic recession or depression might negatively affect your results.

Your Success or Lack of It

Your success in using the information or strategies provided in this book depends on a variety of factors. The Author and the Publisher have no way of knowing how well you will do because they do not know you, your background, your work ethic, your dedication, your motivation, your desire, or your business skills or practices. Therefore, neither the Author nor the Publisher guarantees or implies that you will get rich, that you will do as well, or that you will have any earnings (whether monetary or advertising credits, whether convertible to cash or not), at all.

Businesses and earnings derived therefrom involve unknown risks and are not suitable for everyone. You may not rely on any information presented in this book or otherwise provided by the Author or the Publisher, unless you do so with the knowledge and understanding that you can experience significant losses (including, but not limited to, the loss of any monies paid to purchase this book and/or any monies spent setting up, operating, and/or marketing your business activities, and further, that you may have no earnings at all (whether monetary or advertising credits, whether convertible to cash or not).

Forward-Looking Statements

Materials in this book may contain information that includes or is based upon forward-looking statements within the meaning of the securities litigation reform act of 1995. Forward-looking statements give the Author's expectations or forecasts of future events. You can identify these statements by the fact that they do not relate strictly to historical or current facts. They use words such as "anticipate," "estimate," "expect," "project," "intend," "plan," "believe," and other words and terms of similar meaning in connection with a description of potential earnings or financial performance.

Any and all forward-looking statements here or on any materials in this book are intended to express an opinion of earnings potential. Many factors will be important in determining your actual results and no guarantees are made that you will achieve results similar to the Author or anybody else. In fact, no guarantees are made that you will achieve any results from applying the Author's ideas, strategies, and tactics found in this book.

Purchase Price

Although the Publisher believes the price is fair for the value that you receive, you understand and agree that the purchase price for this book has been arbitrarily set by the Publisher. This price bears no relationship to objective standards.

Due Diligence

You are advised to do your own due diligence when it comes to making any decisions. Use caution and seek the advice of qualified professionals before acting upon the contents of this book or any other information. You shall not consider any examples, documents, or other content in this book or otherwise provided by the Author or Publisher to be the equivalent of professional advice.

The Author and the Publisher assume no responsibility for any losses or damages resulting from your use of any link, information, or opportunity contained in this book or within any other information disclosed by the Author or the Publisher in any form whatsoever.

YOU SHOULD ALWAYS CONDUCT YOUR OWN INVESTIGATION (PERFORM DUE DILIGENCE) BEFORE BUYING PRODUCTS OR SERVICES FROM ANYONE OFFLINE OR VIA THE INTERNET. THIS INCLUDES PRODUCTS AND SERVICES SOLD VIA HYPERLINKS EMBEDDED IN THIS BOOK.

Printed in Great Britain
by Amazon

26195010R00096